Your Towns and Cities in the Great War

Barrow-in-Furness
in the Great War

D1612541

Dedication

For my dad, the late John Tyson Mansergh (school teacher), my granddad, Peter William Weightman (1920–2005). Also in memory of the late Sally Sykes (née Tyson) of High Nibthwaite and Kirkby-in-Furness, whose husband Charlie worked for Burlington Slate.

Your Towns and Cities in the Great War

Barrow-in-Furness in the Great War

Ruth Mansergh

Pen & Sword
MILITARY

First published in Great Britain in 2015 by
PEN & SWORD MILITARY
an imprint of
Pen and Sword Books Ltd
47 Church Street
Barnsley
South Yorkshire S70 2AS

Copyright © Ruth Mansergh, 2015

ISBN 978 1 78383 111 1

The right of Ruth Mansergh to be identified as the author of
this work has been asserted by her in accordance with the Copyright,
Designs and Patents Act 1988.

A CIP record for this book is available from the British Library

All rights reserved. No part of this book may be reproduced or transmitted
in any form or by any means, electronic or mechanical including
photocopying, recording or by any information storage and retrieval
system, without permission from the Publisher in writing.

Printed and bound in England
by CPI Group (UK) Ltd, Croydon, CR0 4YY

Typeset in Times New Roman by Chic Graphics

Pen & Sword Books Ltd incorporates the imprints of
Pen & Sword Archaeology, Atlas, Aviation, Battleground, Discovery,
Family History, History, Maritime, Military, Naval, Politics, Railways,
Select, Social History, Transport, True Crime, Claymore Press,
Frontline Books, Leo Cooper, Praetorian Press, Remember When,
Seaforth Publishing and Wharncliffe.

For a complete list of Pen and Sword titles please contact
Pen and Sword Books Limited
47 Church Street, Barnsley, South Yorkshire, S70 2AS, England
E-mail: enquiries@pen-and-sword.co.uk
Website: www.pen-and-sword.co.uk

Contents

Author Biography

Ruth Mansergh is a full-time mother of two who has worked as a journalist and as a freelance sub-editor/proofreader. She has a degree in English with Social History from Leeds University. Ruth has a long-standing interest in the history of the north of England inherited from her father and grandfather, especially in the history of Cumbria, the area where she was brought up.

Preface

This book reveals how vital Barrow's industrial output was to the 1914–1918 war effort. It also uncovers little-known stories of Barrovians and men from the surrounding area who served in the armed forces, as well as the area's wartime heroines. It is designed to be accessible to all, and for this reason it includes background information on the growth of Barrow. It also acts as a reference guide to local First World War soldiers and includes information on vessels built at Barrow both before and during the war.

Ruth Mansergh, 2014

CHAPTER 1

The War Effort in Barrow

Where the Lakes Meet the Sea

Industrial towns lie on the coastal lowland to the west and south-west of the high fells of the Lake District. Not all of them are ugly, nor were their builders entirely lacking in vision. Leaving the beaten track behind, we will discover, commemorate and reflect on the impact of Great War on the relatively isolated, planned town of Barrow-in-Furness. The town was originally situated within the county of Lancashire (from 1974, it has been part of Cumbria) and until 1780 it was a hamlet, consisting of just five farmhouses.

Germany invaded Belgium, Britain's ally, on 4 August 1914, forcing Britain to declare war in support of vulnerable Belgium. War had come to Barrow and the town's docks, airship sheds and other sensitive areas were immediately placed out of bounds to casual visitors. Barrow traders strove to give the impression that it was business as usual, and notices saying as much were displayed in shop windows. No one wanted to contemplate the possibility of the war lasting beyond Christmas.

Yet, thousands of local men went on to fight and Barrow gained a garrison, while its industrial output soared. The course of the First World War was determined as much by the work done in Britain's factories as by the fighting carried out on the battlefields. Thousands of women came to Barrow, and many other factory towns, to help make munitions. Local women too did their bit for the war effort as munitionettes, as well as driving trams and working as farm labourers, with many enjoying a disposable income for the first time.

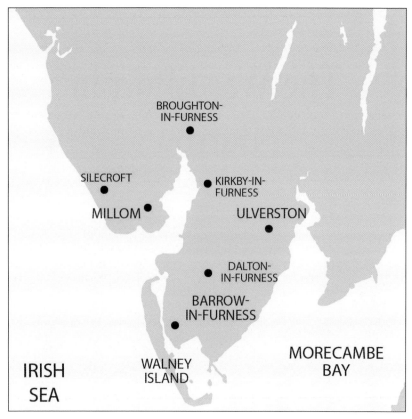

Highlights of the Barrow area include Walney Island and Coniston Water.

Airships, among them the famous *Mayfly*, were built in Barrow during the First World War, while the town's production of naval vessels, including submarines also rapidly accelerated, and the local steelworks saw an upturn in trade. Barrow's shipyard is situated on Barrow Island and is now run by BAE Systems Maritime, yet it is still referred to locally by the name of its previous owner, Vickers Ltd.

Vickers Ltd was formed in Sheffield by the miller Edward Vickers as a steel foundry in 1828. The company went public in 1867 as Vickers, Sons & Company and it produced its first artillery piece in 1890. Meanwhile, William Ashburner, the first Barrow shipbuilder, established a yard in 1847 on a site now covered by the Devonshire Dock Hall and then moved to Hindpool, bordered by Barrow Island, in 1865. The last Ashburner ship to be completed, in 1884, was a schooner, *J&M Garratt*.

The Iron Shipbuilding Company was founded in 1871 by Sir James Ramsden. On registering the new company in 1872, he changed the name to the Barrow Ship Building Company. Barrow shipyard received its first order from the British Admiralty in 1877. The shipyard earned a growing reputation for high quality naval ships and in 1888, having bought out the gun interests of the Maxim Nordenfelt Guns and Ammunition Company, it was renamed the Naval Construction and Armaments Company. The company was created to consolidate the shipbuilding efforts in Barrow and focus these efforts on making warships at a time of pan-European arms escalation.

In 1897, Vickers bought the Barrow Shipbuilding Company and its subsidiary the Maxim Nordenfelt Guns and Ammunition Company, becoming Vickers, Sons and Maxim, Limited. The shipyard at Barrow became the Naval Construction Yard. In 1911, the company was renamed Vickers Ltd Ordnance and ammunition made during this period, including World War One, was stamped 'V.S.M'.

Housing for Industrial Workers
Barrow Island has not been an island since the 1980s, when part of the Devonshire Dock was filled in to provide land for the building of Devonshire Dock Hall, or 'Maggie's Farm'. Over on Walney Island, over Walney Bridge (officially known as the Jubilee Bridge), Vickers Ltd built

Connecting Barrow: Walney Bridge, c. 1910 began the process of merging Walney into a suburb of Barrow. (By kind permission.)

Abbey Road, Barrow-in-Furness

Valentine's Series

Days gone by: Postcard, c.1919 showing the Abbey Road/Dalton Road crossroads in Barrow, with a tram in the distance.

Vickerstown, a planned estate for the company's workers, in 1898. It was described in publicity at the time as a 'model marine garden city'.

Abbey Road is the principal road through central Barrow, while Duke Street is home to two squares: Ramsden Square, with a commemorative memorial to Sir James Ramsden, and Schneider Square. Sir James Ramsden (1822–1896) was a British civil engineer and he played a dominant role in the development of the new town of Barrow. He was also a qualified train driver and became locomotive superintendent for the new Furness Railway Company in January 1846, soon rising to become company secretary, and later serving as managing director between 1866 and 1895. He was also elected to five successive terms as mayor, from 1867 onwards, and lived at Abbotswood, a large new mansion on the outskirts of the town, which he rented from the railway company.

Before the First World War, men working in all the main Barrow industries dealt with large, unwieldy and potentially lethal pieces of metal; they encountered risk and danger on an everyday basis. In 1881, for example, a stoker at the Furness Railway Company, George Francis Driver, was run over and killed by an engine whilst shunting some wagons. He was 20 years of age. The jury brought in a verdict of accidental death and exonerated all those connected with the accident from any blame. Only

The commemorative memorial to Sir James Ramsden situated in Ramsden Square, Barrow. (Taken by author, 2013.)

the factory foremen wore hard hats at this time and the families of miners lived under the constant shadow of calamity, great or small.

On the outbreak of war, Barrovians began to face new dangers, especially those who went to sea. Barrow men were aboard HMS *Amphion*, the first warship lost in the war (sunk by a mine on 6 August 1914), and HMS *Ascot*, the very last British warship to be sunk (torpedoed by German submarine *U-67* off the Farne Islands on 10 November 1918, the day before the announcement of the Armistice). First World War submariners and merchant navy seamen from Barrow are also represented on war memorials in the town.

HMS Amphion *became the first British vessel to be lost at sea during the First World War, when it was sunk by a German mine on 6 August 1914, resulting in over 150 deaths.*

CHAPTER 2

Migration:
The Rise of Barrow

The dramatic growth of Barrow from the late nineteenth to the early twentieth century was fuelled by the ready availability of Furness iron ore. The town's first docks, the Devonshire Docks, opened in 1867 on Barrow Island, allowing the locally produced steel to be put to another use in shipbuilding. The ironworks, steelworks, Devonshire Docks and yards of the Barrow Iron Ship Building Company all required a huge influx of skilled workers to support them.

Barrow shipyard, 1890.

Barrow Iron Works, pictured in the early 1900s: Barrow Haematite/Hematite Steel Co established ironworks (closed in 1963) and steelworks (closed in 1983), separated by the Furness Railway mainline.

Sculpture at Barrow's Dock Museum: Barrow owes its existence to iron ore. (Taken by the author, 2013.)

First the Cornish and Welsh came to work in the mines. Roose Village, Barrow was built around the 1870s to house these miners, most of them former tin miners from Cornwall. Then came the iron and steel workers from Staffordshire and the Midlands, soon joined by engineering and shipbuilding workers from Scotland, Tyneside and Belfast. Skilled and unskilled labourers involved in the shipbuilding business also poured into the town.

In 1870, the Barrow and Calcutta Jute Company, a jute and flax mill, was founded. A year later, the company was putting up tenements in Hindpool, bordered by Barrow Island, in a style that would have been familiar to many of the Scottish workers who lived in them. The Scotch Buildings, which once housed up to 1,000 people, were demolished in 1956.

The Devonshire Buildings, two adjacent apartment buildings in Barrow Island, were also constructed between 1872 and 1875 to house workers at the docks and the yards. Similar tenements exist across Barrow Island. A photograph of inhabitants of the Devonshire Buildings taken around 1900, (which is reproduced in Elizabeth Roberts's book *Working Class Barrow*

Photograph taken in the early 1900s of Ship Street Tenement (now a listed building), on Barrow Island, one of four identical blocks set to the rear of the sandstone Devonshire Buildings.

and Lancaster, 1890 to 1930), suggests that, for some impoverished local children, wearing a hat may have been more usual than wearing shoes. In 1873 the Barrow Iron Shipbuilding Company put up rows of wooden huts to the south of Barrow Island, intended to house 3,000 workers. These huts were condemned in 1877.

The Egerton Buildings, two U-shaped blocks on Barrow Island, were constructed for Furness Railway Company Workers between 1879 and 1884. Shipyard workers not lucky enough to be housed in the tenement blocks or huts were forced to live aboard the liner SS *Alaska*, which was moored in Barrow docks until she was broken up in 1902. During a 20-month period in 1908–1909, a soup kitchen in the iron and steel works area of Hindpool estimated that it had fed two million people. The soup kitchens were relied upon by many of the town's poorest men, women and children.

The planned Vickerstown estate built on Walney Island by Vickers Ltd in 1898, was prompted by a lack of housing for the shipyard workers. It was the first local working-class estate to have electric lighting and to consist of homes that were built to last. A ferry service operated by the Furness Railway Company transported residents to work and over to Barrow.

Egerton Buildings on Barrow Island were designed by Paley & Austin and erected by Smith and Caird of Dundee, working on behalf of the Furness Railway Company.

Mikasa Street, Vickerstown in 1901. The street was named after the Japanese battleship Mikasa, *which was built in Barrow. After the First World War, Vickerstown houses began to be sold to tenants.*

The Ferry Road Triangle of terraced housing stock on Barrow Island was built in the late nineteenth century and has no garden space. Yet, Barrow had no back-to-back houses in blind alleys, like other industrial areas of Britain. In 1913 100 new houses were completed in Delhi Street and Dominion Street, Walney Island as part of the south Vickerstown 'infill' development. The houses were financed by Vickers.

The 'D' streets, where street names begin with the letter D – Dunvegan, Dundee, for example – and the 'A' streets of the Cavendish Park Estate, Barrow Island were completed in 1914. The land, which was severely limited, had been purchased from the Furness Railway Company and was developed by Vickers in collaboration with the town council for the company's workers.

Housing Barrow's Wartime Workforce
Personnel numbers at the Barrow Vickers works increased in 1914. Within two months of the outbreak of hostilities, Vickers secured a War Office loan for the purchase of land on Walney. By the summer of 1916, the

Hearth and rivetters: Ships used to be rivetted (they have been welded since the 1940s). The rivetters' hearth shows what it would have been like to heat up the rivets and then bash them into the rivetting seams. (Photo taken at Dock Museum by author, summer 2013)

The Dock Museum at Barrow-in-Furness preserves the town's shipbuilding heritage. (Photo taken by author, 2013)

company had built a total of 610 three-bedroom houses, and subsidised the building of another 111 by private syndicates.

In 1915 and 1916, a member of the Government committee on poor time-keeping visited Barrow. His reports indicated concern about the possible effects of drunkenness on industrial production, but he apparently concluded that alcoholism was not a serious issue in Barrow. Of far more significance was the shortage of accommodation for workers.

A hostel for 110 female munition workers arriving in Barrow from other towns was erected on Walney Island. It was well furnished, even equipped with writing and reading rooms. By summer 1916, the Salvation Army had opened another hostel in Barrow, housing 250 female munitions workers, and Trades Hostels Ltd, in which Vickers held a controlling interest, had built a hostel for 230 men on Barrow Island. For single men who preferred the comforts of a private home, Vickers altered and furnished Bankfield Boarding House in Barrow, which accommodated 80 men. The Ramsden Hotel also provided comfortable quarters for the manageresses and forewomen employed at Vickers.

Public houses and hotels attempted to make up for financial losses resulting from new liquor rules announced on 7 July 1915, by letting out spare rooms to munitions workers. The rules, which applied within a 10-mile radius of Barrow and included Dalton, Askam and Millom, placed restrictions on opening hours and even banned customers from buying rounds of drinks.

The Parliamentary Commission on Industrial Unrest paid a visit to Barrow in the summer of 1917. It examined overcrowding, the worst example being the conditions found at a house in Melbourne Street, where twelve adults and seven children occupied a single three-bedroom house. It also detected a deep-rooted fear of eviction among the town's population. Resentment was further exacerbated by the fact that a small but significant number of Belgian refugees had been brought to work in Barrow.

Some of the refugees had, in time, bought houses, subsequently applying for warrants to evict the sitting tenants. A local magistrate told the commission: 'This is a very sore point. As sure as you and I are there, there will be Satan's row if Belgian people are allowed to buy houses and the working classes of Barrow-in-Furness are turned out into the streets. There will be a riot.'

The commissioners called the housing situation in Barrow a 'crying scandal'. After threats of strike action by the town's shipyard workers, the Government finally intervened. Tenants were at last given proper protection from unscrupulous landlords – as long as they upheld the conditions of their tenancy agreements – and Barrow was designated a 'special area', in which the building of new, temporary accommodation for workers was to be urgently undertaken.

Belgian Refugees Arrive in Barrow

In mid-January 1915, it was announced that Millom, a town across the Duddon Estuary with a pre-First World War population of 10,000 (reduced to 7,132 by the 2001 Census), was expected to receive between 300 and 500 Belgian refugees, who would work at Barrow Shipyard. The arrangements to accommodate them in the town were made by the Millom Ratepayers' Association. There were ex-soldiers among the refugees, who had been interned at Flushing in Holland and many had been forced to work for the Germans. A special workmen's train was laid on from Millom to Barrow with around 500 seats. However, the train was unheated and their uncomfortable commute led many of the Belgians to move to Barrow.

The refugees soon began taking part in the life of Millom, for instance on 28 January 1915, an Anglo-Belgian concert was given at the local Drill Hall. One Belgian then living on Albert Street with his wife and son, Dubosch Heliodore, became a local hero on 27 March 1915. A horse pulling a manure cart belonging to Millom Co-op came loose when the shaft of the cart broke. It was careering through the town when Heliodore pluckily managed to stop it.

In April 1915, it was noted that there were 640 workmen, mainly Belgians travelling from Millom to Vickers every day. Around 70 more Belgians had arrived by the end of July 1915, bringing the Belgian population in the town up to 600. Among the later arrivals was a Belgian teacher who began teaching at St James' School in Millom. They were joined by a few Dutch refugees within two years. Some stayed only a short time, like the Millom Belgians who emigrated to the Belgian Congo, where they had found work, in January 1916. Three years later, on 17 January 1919, the first 20 Belgians left Millom to return home.

Post-war Slump: Hanging Around the Streets

While the wages of many of Barrow's workers rose during the war, particularly among those in the shipyard, and the expansion of employment opportunities for women raised families' living standards, its end brought about a catastrophic depression. The 1919 Restoration of Pre-War Practices Act forced many women to leave their wartime roles, as soldiers came home and factories switched to peacetime production.

In Barrow, free school meals were introduced in 1919 in response to the economic downturn. Early in 1921, ship orders began to be cancelled. Within Vickers, by 1922 the technical and clerical staff seem to have been as badly affected by unemployment as the workers. Barrow's Co-operative Society also had to shed a large proportion of its retail staff.

In 1913, the town's population was 65,257, increasing to 83,179 by 1918. Just one year later, almost 10,000 people had left the town, and Barrow's population continued to fall, shrinking by around 10 per cent between 1921 and 1931. It lost a considerable portion of young adults and their families, who very often emigrated or moved to areas of Britain with more employment opportunities.

The birthrate figures for Barrow reveal a marked decline between 1920 and 1930, which supports the view that the working classes began to plan their families around the time of the First World War. However, smaller households also meant more food to go around in times of hardship.

CHAPTER 3

Barrow Folk and the War Effort

On the outbreak of the war in August 1914, the King's Own Royal Lancaster Regiment was made up of two Regular and two Territorial Battalions, as well as a Special Reserve Battalion. The 1st/4th Battalion was mobilised at Barrow on 4 August 1914 and returned to England in April 1919.

We Think You Ought to Go
An advert from the *Barrow Guardian* (15 August 1914) reads 'Your King and Country Need You'. A second, published just a fortnight later, is more urgent and simply states 'Recruits Wanted'. In only 14 days, the recruitment demographic had expanded from men aged 19 to 30 to include those aged from 17 to 45.

There certainly was a lot of patriotic fervour in Barrow in the early days of the war, fuelled by enthusiastic pieces in the local press. In August and September 1914, there are regular newspaper reports of men being recruited, almost as if there was some form of unofficial battle between the localities to see who could provide the most recruits – a form of civic pride, no doubt. Initially, there were also recruiting drives by regiments who specifically chose these locations, and this creates, at first glance, puzzling enlistment patterns. For example, in Millom (Cumberland) two particularly active recruiting regiments were the East Lancashire Regiment and the Royal Dublin Fusiliers, neither of which had any geographical affiliation with the area. Several of their recruits subsequently died in the war.

The *Barrow News* also regularly printed critical letters from serving soldiers, who would caustically refer to un-enlisted men as 'slackers'. The pressure to join up was all too evident.

Hold the Clarkes in Honour

Whole families were soon separated by the war, such as the Clarkes of Millom. Six of seven eligible male members of the Clarke family enlisted, leaving wives and 14 children in total.

***Barrow News*, 12 June 1915**:

We are enabled to present the photographs of members of a family which has displayed worthy patriotism and self-sacrifice in connection with the war. They are Mrs. Clark [sic] (formerly Mrs. W. Clark), of 6, Lonsdale Terrace, Millom, and the five members

*The six serving soldiers in the Clarke family from Milliom were held up as an example to the young single 'slackers'. (*Barrow News*, 12 June 1915)*

of her family who, since the war broke out, have left home and kith and kin, and are now gallantly serving their King and Country in the military forces.

Private Edwin Clarke, who left his home in Wales and volunteered for service with the 1st Border Regt., is now fighting the Dardanelles: he left a wife and 5 children in order to do so. Private Thomas Clarke is serving in the Northumberland Fusiliers; and Lance-Corporal Barker Clarke and Corporal Ernest Clarke, both of the 4th King's Own Royal Lancaster Regt., are at the time of writing helping to uphold the honour of England in the trenches 'somewhere in France'. With them also is Private Solomon Richardson, the husband of Mrs White's granddaughter.

A striking example of patriotism was given by Mrs. White's elder son, William Edward Clarke. He was formerly in the Coldstream Guards, and went through the Boer War, for which he holds the medals. One of them has six bars (the highest number attainable), denoting the battles in which he fought. When the present war broke out he was living in Canada. Though his term as a reservist had long expired, he threw up his job and hastened to England, hoping to rejoin his old and famous regiment, which has done so nobly in the great conflict with the Huns. He has, however, the hardest of luck, for on presenting himself for examination he was found to be medically unfit through suffering from varicose veins.

Altogether, out of seven male members of the family, six have either served or are serving with the colours. It is worthy of note that those who are now away, having answered their country's call, are all married men, and altogether they have left 14 children behind them. What an example they have set to the young single 'slackers', who have no such responsibilities, but who allow such men to fight for them.

Three days after this report was published, on 15 June 1915, Sergeant Barker Clarke, 1st/4th Battalion King's Own Royal Lancaster Regiment, of Millom, was killed in action near Rue d'Ouvert, at the age of 31. He was a member of the original Volunteer Force, as he had enlisted prior to April 1908, and was already serving when the Territorial Force (TF) was formed on 1 April 1908.

CHAPTER 4

Barrow Needs its Workers

Barrow sent 3,313 men to war from a population of 72,360 – a small proportion compared to many other towns throughout the rest of the country. However, Barrow was a major producer of war materials and needed to retain skilled workers.

Around 200 men in the local Territorial Force unit, the 4th Battalion, King's Own Royal Lancaster Regiment, were employed in key industries. Among them was Private Edward John Cowley, who was mobilised on the declaration of war, then within a month sent back to Vickers to work on munitions as a coppersmith. He died in 1921, aged 24, and is buried in Dalton Cemetery.

Since the Territorial Force was responsible for recruiting its own men, the corollary of this was that the local battalion was undermanned, as sufficient recruits could not be found to bring it up to wartime establishment. The County Association – the body responsible for the administration of the Territorial Force – tried to solve the problem by setting up a second-line battalion at Blackpool, specifically to recruit and train men to augment the ranks of the newly-designated 1st/4th Battalion. However, this measure only had limited success due to competition from other regiments, all equally keen to have their pick of recruits.

Vickers Ltd
The 1911 Census listed 5,935 men employed in general engineering and 4,297 employed in ship construction in Barrow, comprising nearly half of

the town's male workforce of 22,363. By contrast, only 1,485 were employed in the manufacture of iron and steel. Vickers Ltd workers broke up for their summer holidays in the last week of July 1914, but they were soon back in harness. Four years of wartime discipline lay ahead, as the Vickers Barrow works effectively came under Government control for the duration of the war.

Miners

Other communities in the district also needed key workers. In places such as Askam in Furness, Ulverston, Dalton in Furness and Millom, industrial labour was concentrated into either mining iron ore or processing it into iron and steel. Naturally, this utilised a lot of skilled labour and employers, worried about production and profits, were loth to lose their men to the armed forces as the country moved to a war footing. The Government agreed that many skilled workers could better serve their country in the mines and foundries, rather than on the Front Line.

Agricultural Workers

Agriculture still forms a sizeable proportion of the south Lakeland economy. A considerable number of local men who joined the armed forces started their working lives as farm servants. Others were the children of coal and ore miners, who were often treated almost as indentured serfs by their employers. In return for heavy work, they received little more than their board and lodgings. It is not surprising that many farm servants would have regarded the war as an opportunity to escape their impoverished existence.

A farmer wishing to employ new labourers or servants would attend one of the local hiring fairs held at Whitsuntide and Martinmas. Girls, as well as boys, went to find work at the hirings. The following is a an account of a hiring fair from *Lakeland Dalesfolk, 1900-1935* by W.R. Mitchell: 'At Ulverston, lads just stood around on the side of the streets. If a farmer thought someone looked like a big lump of cheap labour, he'd go and see if he could hire him for as little as he could.'

Large houses in the area also employed many servant girls. In Kentmere (a few miles away from Kendal), servants mostly came from Barrow; some of them later became farmers' wives.

At the beginning of the war, relatively few farmers joined up. But, after conscription was introduced in 1916, there was a shortage of farm labour, as workers were needed for military service. As far as the army was concerned, agricultural workers were a valuable resource at the Front. Many of them had considerable experience of handling horses, including heavy draught horses. These animals were the mainstay of army transport and huge numbers of men in various corps were needed to look after and manage them.

In *Cumbria, Within Living Memory*, a collection of oral history accounts collected by the Cumbria Federation of Women's Institutes, a farmer, then in his eighties, recalled farming in the years after the First World War. He felt it had been in a poor way – not much profit and very hard work: 'Men coming out of the Forces after the war with a little bit of gratuity – many of them ex-farmworkers – would get a small-holding, hoping to settle and make it pay. They didn't last three years – it was very sad.'

CHAPTER 5

Coastal Targets

Barrow was the scene of a staged invasion in August 1910. A force of mock invaders were given the task of landing on Walney and capturing Walney Bridge and the shipyard. Perhaps it suited the military that the invaders succeeded, as the event was used to prove the vulnerability of England's industrial centres – thus encouraging more Government funding for the armed forces. More than 5,000 troops took part that day, with their activities providing some unexpected free entertainment for hoards of Barrovians.

Manned until 2003, Walney Island Lighthouse dates from 1804. It replaced an earlier wooden structure of 1790, which burned down the previous year.

U-boat Attack on Walney Island

German Commander Otto Hersing had been selected for the task of extending the zone of German submarine operations into the western waters of England. On 21 January 1915, he and his crew set sail on *U-21*, travelling through the Straits of Dover by night, then proceeding across the whole length of the English Channel. *U-21* turned north and passed the Welsh coast into the Irish Sea, becoming the first enemy submarine ever to have done so.

To the surprise of the local garrison, *U-21* appeared off Walney Island on 29 January. A U-boat was sighted in the Irish Sea, on the surface in broad daylight, at about 2pm, in fairly shallow water some 2 to 3 miles off Walney. The ship was taking her time and the soldiers on shore could not ascertain her nationality – Barrow was, after all, a place where numerous British submarines were built or taken to be repaired. Was this among the latter? It was a bold move for the vessel to proceed to and fro on the surface in broad daylight.

Barrow News, 30 January 1915:

Forty minutes passed before her hostility could be determined, but Commander Otto Hersing now opened fire on the airship shed at Walney. Two shots were fired from a gun that she had aboard, but both missiles fell short. The Walney guns replied and, after discharging about a dozen rounds, sunk the enemy's craft. The action of the batteries could be felt in the houses on Barrow Island – which are a good distance away from the fort. Under ordinary circumstances when

Otto Hersing was known amongst his colleagues as the 'Zerstörer der Schlachtschiffe', destroyer of battleships. His first victim was HMS *Pathfinder.*

U-21 is pictured here, on the far right.

Fort Walney, pictured here in 1940, is thought to have been the target of enemy submarine U-21 in January 1915. (By kind permission)

any firing practice was contemplated at the fort, the inhabitants of the Island were invariably informed in order that they might open windows to obviate any damage in that direction, also to allay any possible alarm.

The fort at Walney was manned by No 7 Company of the Lancashire and Cheshire Royal Garrison Artillery (RGA). The men of the RGA were overjoyed at the opportunity to engage in warfare at close quarters, and with such notable success. The military authorities chose not comment on the incident, yet the fact remains that a German submarine was fired upon from the Walney Fort. However, the vessel seems not to have been sunk by gunfire but to have merely submerged herself.

The *U-21* survived the war and, still under Hersing's command, was accidentally sunk on 22 February 1919 in the North Sea, while under tow by a British warship. Some accounts maintain that she was deliberately scuttled by Hersing.

U-24 Off Lowca

A similar incident occurred a few months later further up the coast from Walney. On Monday, 16 August 1915, the *U-24* surfaced at 4.50 am off Lowca, a small village on the West Cumbrian coast (then known as Cumberland). *U-24* was one of three U-boats operating in the Irish Sea around that date. *U-27* and *U-38* were positioned off Llandudno as part of a plan to pick up German officers escaping from Aled Duffryn, a camp in North Wales.

The *U-24*'s Commander, Kapitanleutnant Rudolf Schneider, had already sunk HMS *Formidable* during the very first German underwater attack at night, on 1 January 1915 off Portland Bill, Dorset. He would later nearly bring America into the war, when he torpedoed passenger ship SS *Arabic* on 19 August 1915, 50 miles south of Kinsale, County Cork, with the loss of 44 lives, including three American citizens.

Rudolf Schneider (1882– 1917): On 13 October 1917, during very stormy weather, Schneider was lost overboard from the conning tower of U-87.

The *U-24* entered Parton Bay, fired some ranging shots and stopped the engines about a mile off the village of Lowca, which was then a hive of heavy industry, largely based upon coal extraction and iron production. The captain directed the boat's gunners to bombard the coke ovens and toluene plants of the 'top secret' Workington Iron and Steel Company (ironically, the plant had been installed by the German manufacturer Koppers). The Lowca plant was targeted because it manufactured synthetic toluene out of benzene, which was then used to make explosives.

A total of 55 shells out of the submarine's magazine of 300 were aimed at the works in 55 minutes, but for such a daring effort, the rewards were small: 30 hits were recorded on the works, but only four did any damage. A 50 gallon drum of Benzol was set ablaze, with the fire quickly spreading to the loading tanks, and two 11,000 gallon Naphtha tanks were perforated, although they did not ignite. The powerhouse had also been hit with a dud shell and its chimney was left with a hole in it; 900 windows were also broken.

However, the owners of the works had a well-rehearsed wartime emergency plan in force. If the works came under attack from Zeppelins or warships, certain valves and steam traps were to be fully opened and six blasts given on the steam whistle, warning the villagers to flee. The valve operator, Mr Oscar Ohlson, released flaming gas into the atmosphere, which produced a great cloud of smoke – this seems to have convinced the Germans that a vital target had been hit. The U-boat then submerged.

No one was injured, although a dog called Lion was hit by a stray shell splinter. William Twentyman, a stationmaster and goods agent at Parton, just north of Whitehaven, held back a Whitehaven-bound passenger train at his station until the shelling had stopped.

Afterwards, the full force of local anger fell upon Mrs Hildegarde Burnyeat (née Retzlaff) the German wife of former Liberal MP and barrister William John Dalzell Burnyeat, who lived at Moresby House. Mrs Burnyeat, the daughter of a Prussian army officer, remained pro-German throughout the war and in the wake of the U-boat raid she was arrested by the authorities under the Defence of the Realm Act and interned at Aylesbury Prison in Buckinghamshire. She was still in prison when her husband died a year later, aged just 42, though she was allowed to visit him during his last hours.

After his death, Mrs Burnyeat was released from internment and allowed to live with an English family in Harrogate, causing some antagonism in the North Yorkshire town. What happened to Mrs Burnyeat subsequently is not clear. She had no children and may have chosen to be exchanged and returned to Germany. However, she was not the only local with German connections to come under suspicion. During the early months of the war Barrow was swept with spy fever: an Austrian dental technician was falsely arrested and families with vaguely Germanic-sounding names became targets of blind prejudice.

One of the best contemporary accounts of the Lowca raid is a poem entitled 'The Bombardment of the Cumberland Coast' by Joseph Holmes of Siddick (1859–1930), who was then a stationmaster on the Lowca railway line. It was sold on handbills for one penny, with the promise that 'Proceeds of sale will be given to the Soldiers' Tobacco Fund'.

> *On August Sixteenth, old Kaiser Bill*
> *Said to his men, 'Now prove your skill,*
> *And try and reach the Cumberland coast,*
> *The feat of which I'd like to boast.'*
>
> *The Kaiser's word they did obey,*
> *And fired away in Parton Bay,*
> *With shot and shell they did their best*
> *To put the Lowca works to rest.*

The damage done was not so much,
The Benzol plant they did not touch,
One shell fell here, another there
Which gave the workmen quite a scare.

The inhabitants too grew quite alarmed,
Because this port is still unarmed,
This opportunity the enemy seized,
And rained the shells just where he pleased.

Two shells went through a cottage home,
The father shouts 'A German Bomb,'
The children then ran out like bees,
And joined the Lowca refugees.

The submarine then made its way
Across the dub from Parton Bay,
To find some other defenceless port
Where German fiends could have their sport.

Remember Bill the time will come
When we'll have thee beneath our thumb
And thou wilt wish thou had'st never been born
For we'll treat thee with the utmost scorn.

They barbarous deeds and acts are such
We could not punish thee too much.
Don't ask from us to be forgiven
The most fiendish villain under heaven.

Barrow Garrison

As a strategically important location, Barrow warranted its own protective garrison. In the first couple of weeks of war, this was provided by the mobilisation of the Territorial Force – the 4th King's Own Royal Lancaster Regiment, the members of which were billeted in the town and environs, and were constantly on guard against possible acts of sabotage. It was envisaged as a home defence force for service during wartime, yet any member or unit of the force could volunteer for overseas service.

Parton Bay: An important sea port that was completely washed away in the 1700s. Lowca has long consigned heavy industry to the past. (Copyright John Holmes)

Very little information about the Barrow Garrison survives; the most fruitful source of information can be found on the war graves in Barrow Cemetery. By listing these men's details chronologically, you can see the pattern emerging as different regiments moved in and out of the town during the war. Naturally enough, there were casualties amongst the men of the garrison due to accidents and natural causes and some of these men were buried at Barrow. Initially, the Barrow Garrison would have been billeted on the local population, before more permanent camps could be established. There was also a camp at Ramsden Dock and one at Cavendish Park.

The War Office decided that a more professional force was needed and the vanguard of the official Barrow-in-Furness Garrison was provided by the 4th (Extra Reserve) Battalion, Lancashire Fusiliers, who arrived in late August and early September 1914. On being exposed to the presence of Regular soldiers – rather than the 'weekend soldiers' of the Territorial Force – many more local men were enticed to join their ranks and there were a substantial number of enlistments.

During this time, the local press reported a colourful story about a young officer who got into trouble on the Home Front. Trafford Leigh-

Mallory would later go on to be one of the key figures in the 1940 Battle of Britain, but during the First World War he was among the officers of the 4th Battalion Lancashire Fusiliers stationed at Barrow.

Under the headline 'A Lieutenant Fined', the *Barrow News* of 16 January 1915 reported that Lieutenant Trafford Leigh-Mallory was summoned for not having registered a motor car. Harry Smith, dealer in cars, of Cornwallis Street, said that he had sold a car to the officer. It was not registered and he told the officer that registration would be required. A local policeman, PC Cox, spoke of seeing the car outside a picture palace one evening and noticing the Lieutenant drive away in it.

Air Chief Marshall: Trafford Leigh-Mallory was killed on 14 November 1944, whilst en route to Ceylon to take up the post of Air Commander-in-Chief South East Asia Command, when his aircraft crashed over the French Alps.

A letter was read from the defendant, stating that his military duties prevented him from attending at court. The Chief Constable remarked that altogether the defendant could have been charged with four offences. He had also brought the car to the picture palace and asked a constable to look after it while he was inside. The constable had told him he could not do so, and the officer replied, 'Oh! It's all right; I have left it before,' before heading into the picture palace. A fine of 20 shillings and costs was imposed.

Flags at Half-Mast – a Military Funeral

The Commander of the Barrow Garrison, Frederick Clifton Briggs, 3rd Battalion, Border Regiment, lived in an imposing house in Prospect Road. He did not survive the war, however. Frederick Clifton died on 30 December 1916, aged 59, and was buried at Barrow Cemetery. Members of the garrison were often called upon to provide escort parties for local men who were given military funerals, and this time they found themselves providing an escort for their own Commander.

Barrow News, 6 January 1917:

The profound grief occasioned amongst the military and civic population of Barrow by the somewhat sudden demise of the late Col. F. C. Briggs was demonstrated in a marked degree when the funeral took place on Wednesday afternoon, the body being interred

A military funeral on such a scale as that of Colonel Briggs was a unique spectacle in Barrow. Various units of the Regular Forces were represented, and there was a detachment from the 14th Battalion, Lancashire Volunteer Regiment. There were also contingents of the Royal Navy and Naval Air Service.

in the Borough Cemetery with military honours befitting an officer of such high rank. The late Colonel was Garrison Commander here, but had only succeeded Col. Fryer some two months ago. He passed away early last Saturday morning after a week's illness.

Since then the town had honoured the deceased Colonel by flying flags at half-mast from the Town Hall and various other flag-staffs. During his brief sojourn in Barrow Col. Briggs had won the admiration and appreciation of all with whom he came in contact. He has had a strenuous and distinguished military career having fought in the Afghan, South African and the present war.

The Territorial Forces

Some local men joined the Territorial Forces (TF) and a lot had already become members before the war, because it acted as a social club of sorts. Aside from the comradeship, there was also the opportunity to go away for a fortnight each year to an annual camp, which effectively constituted a paid holiday in the days when such a thing was a rarity. The Territorials had different terms of service to the Regular Army – their primary function was to serve at home in the UK garrisons, thereby releasing regular troops for service overseas.

In the early stages of the war members of the Territorial Forces could not be compelled to serve abroad and they only did so by consent, signing the Imperial Service Obligation. Those who did so were issued with special lapel badges (the Imperial Service Badge), to show that they had volunteered for overseas service and to prevent them from being accused of not doing their bit. A term of service in the Territorials was four years and there are many cases of men whose term expired while they were serving in France, and in this case they were discharged as time-expired. Later, following the Military Service Act, this rule was swept away and the Territorial Forces' members' term of service was for the duration of the war, although the men eligible for discharge got a considerable bounty as a sweetener. Many time-expired men found themselves called up again once conscription was introduced.

Murder at Cavendish Dock
Company Sergeant Major Henry Lynch, 5th (Home Service) Garrison Battalion, Royal Welsh Fusiliers, was murdered at Cavendish Dock during the First World War and is buried at Barrow Cemetery. Thirty-nine-year-old Henry Lynch, who was from Pendarran, Glamorgan had served in the

The Imperial Service Badge was granted to members of the Territorial Forces who had volunteered to serve overseas during the First World War. (By kind permission)

army for 21 years when he died on 13 January 1917, after being shot with a service rifle in a guard room by another soldier. There was no direct evidence of the motive.

A large crowd of people lined the streets of Barrow to watch the funeral procession of Company Sergeant Major Lynch, who was then buried with full military honours. The cortège comprised the band of the South Wales Borderers, and officers representing Barrow Garrison. The murderer who was convicted at the Manchester Assizes, Private Thomas Clinton, is not commemorated by the Commonwealth Graves Commission (CWGC) although, as a serving soldier at the time of his death, he is entitled to be. He was convicted of Lynch's murder and executed at Strangeways Prison in Manchester.

Later on in the war, the military seems to have forgotten this principle of omitting convicted murderers from the CWGC and some early examples of soldiers who were executed by civil courts appear. However, once it was realised that official commemoration would follow automatically, a policy was instituted (initially by the RAF) that such men would be discharged from the service on the day before their execution by civil authority. This meant that they would not qualify for commemoration, as they were technically no longer in the services and their death was not attributable to their war service.

All such executions were for murder, although there is one example of a man executed by the civil authorities for treason, who was not discharged from the army due to some official oversight; consequently his name appears on the Brookwood Memorial in Surrey, in accordance with the rules for commemoration of war dead. The Brookwood Memorial commemorates 3,500 men and women of the land forces of the Commonwealth who died during the First World War and have no known grave, the circumstances of their death being such that they could not appropriately be commemorated on any of the campaign memorials in the various theatres of war. Some died at sea, while travelling on hospital ships and troop transports in waters not associated with the major campaigns, and a few were killed in flying accidents or in aerial combat.

Today Private Clinton is no longer buried within the walls of Strangeways Prison. After the riot in the 1980s, all the burial sites of executed prisoners were dug up during the subsequent renovations. Any living relatives of the deceased men were contacted and asked if they wanted to arrange for the reburial of the remains or to leave it to the Home Office and Prison Service. Unclaimed remains were taken for cremation and re-interred in Blackley Cemetery, Manchester; the remains of Private Thomas Clinton were among them.

Found Drowned

The bodies of two men, Frank Leonard, 21, and an unknown seaman, were discovered washed ashore at Barrow in 1917. Leonard was found on the foreshore at the south end of Biggar Bank. It was later established that they had been killed when their vessel, HMS *Champagne*, was torpedoed off the Isle of Man on 9 October 1917. Frank Leonard, an Able Seaman of the Royal Navy Volunteer Reserve whose parents lived in Surrey, was interred in Barrow Cemetery with naval honours. A verdict of 'Found drowned' was returned at the inquest concerning his death.

Sadly, Leonard and his unknown shipmate were not the only deceased seamen from his vessel to be washed up at Barrow.

Barrow News, **3 November 1917:**

> The body of another seaman washed ashore at Barrow was not identified; a verdict of 'Found drowned' was returned at an inquest. The naval authorities undertook the burial. Harold Allsopp said that whilst walking on the shore at South End, Walney at 4pm on Saturday afternoon, he saw the body of a man and gave information to the police. The only clothing he had was a striped shirt and a waistcoat with brass buttons and a crown and anchor. He appeared to be a naval seaman.

In her wartime role, HMS *Champagne* was armed with two 6-inch guns and two six-pounder guns. In 1917, she was lent to the French navy but retained her British crew. However, she then reverted to the Royal Navy and was on her way from Liverpool to rejoin the rest of her patrol, when, while cruising off the west coast of the Isle of Man on 9 October 1917, she was torpedoed by *U-96*. Captain Percy Brown and 46 of the crew of the vessel landed at Port Erin. After the news had been received at Government Office, a police inspector and a doctor were despatched by car to Port Erin.

At 2pm, the police inspector reported that 50 of the crew had been landed, one of whom was suffering from wounds and another from shock. At 1pm, the Peel lifeboat was launched, and arrangements were made for all fishing vessels lying in Peel Harbour to proceed to the scene of the disaster.

HMS Champagne *was built before the war, and originally known as the SS* Oropesa.

At 3pm, news was received from Port Erin that 150 of the crew had been landed at Port St Mary, and at 5pm the Peel lifeboat returned to Peel with 21 survivors. For the latter, clothing was obtained from Knockaloe Camp, and medical aid was provided. Harbour Master Elliot, of Port Erin, as the local representative of the Shipwrecked Mariners Society, provided clothing for the men landed at the southern ports, and the police inspector arranged for billets for the survivors. The total number reported landed on the island out of the crew of 305 was 217, but some additional survivors were subsequently found.

CHAPTER 6

Railways and Railwaymen Remembered

The railways played a major role in the development of Barrow. The Furness Railway directors first created a railway, then the docks, and subsequently the iron and steelworks, and the shipyard. They also supervised the creation of the town hall.

During the First World War, the Cumbrian railways were required to perform heroic endeavours to move unprecedented volumes of fuel, munitions, troops, and casualties. Trains carrying armaments were also transported, yet at different times, in case they were sabotaged.

The Furness Railway

The Furness Railway existed from 1846 to 1922, becoming part of the London, Midland and Scottish Railway in 1923. The Furness Railway, as originally laid, carried passengers but it was intended principally for slate and iron ore traffic, and when it opened in 1846 it extended from Barrow and Piel to the Dalton and Kirkby lines for freight.

The railway was then extended to Ulverston and opened to freight in April 1854, with passengers following soon after. The Ulverstone (sic) and Lancaster line opened in October 1857, providing the southern outlet for the Furness Railway.

The original main line did not run through Barrow and Barrow Central Station was not opened until 1882. There were other train lines in Barrow, however, such as the line to Ramsden Dock and the branch off that line to the shipyard station. Ramsden Dock Station survived until 1922. The original railway terminus at Piel (in fact on Roa Island) became the end of a branch line from Barrow, with a halt and a station at Rampside. The branch south of Ulverston went to Conishead Station, and this was also kept open during the war. The line to Sandside continued on to the West Coast Main Line, while Furness Railway trains worked through to Kendal.

The First World War found the Furness Railway serving an area that was destined to play a big part in Great Britain's war effort. This encompassed Barrow and the blast furnace plants at Ulverston, Millom and in the Cleator district (West Cumbria), and the Messrs Vickers gun-testing range (established 1897) on the sandhills near Eskmeals, West Cumbria. Eskmeals came under the control of the Ministry of Munitions for the duration of the hostilities and guns were subjected to testing there, before they were sent by rail from sidings to the Bootle line to Barrow for assembly into battleships.

After 12 months of war, the cost of railway wagon renewals was up by £10,000, and usage was also increasing, with no less than 3,000 workmen's tickets issued. Sunday goods workings were introduced, which consisted largely of Admiralty coal specials.

By Armistice Day, a total of 515 men from the Furness Railway had entered the armed forces, which constituted 18 per cent of the staff at the commencement of hostilities. A total of 68 lost their lives during the war.

The Coniston Railway and Coniston Mines
The original Furness Railway extended as far as Broughton-in-Furness. The Coniston Railway, running for 8.5 miles from Coniston to Broughton, with stations at Torver and Woodland opened in 1859, followed by an extension of the line to the copper mines in 1860. Two years later, the Coniston Railway was amalgamated with the Furness Railway and a curve was put in at Foxfield, where lines led in one direction towards Millom, Bootle and Whitehaven and in the other towards Barrow.

Coniston Mines had a brief period of prosperity at the beginning of the First World War, when a new electrolytic copper plant was constructed to reprocess the dumps using electrolysis. However, this plant was short-lived: the principal engineer, Count Henri de Varney, was killed during the war, when his plane was shot down by the Germans in 1915. Mining had completely ceased in the area by the early 1940s.

Towards the end of the First World War, workmen's trains ran between Coniston and Barrow. The Coniston line had already shut by the time Dr

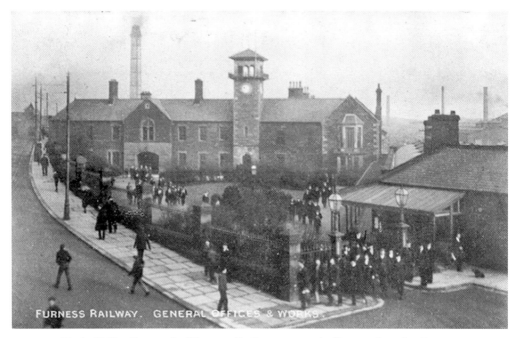

Early 1900s: Postcard of Furness Railway, general offices and works, Barrow. Just as Gorbals tenement builders could apparently influence local architecture, so could railway companies. The Furness Railway Company encouraged a form of brightly patterned brickwork that was locally known as 'the railway style'. (By kind permission)

Beeching came along. It was closed to passengers in 1958 and to freight in 1962.

Millom: A Rich Mining Heritage

When the railway first came to Millom, the local station was called Holborn Hill. Yet, with the opening of the Hodbarrow Iron Works in 1867, streets of black-slate houses began to be shovelled together on the marshy fields as fast as the builders could cart the stone from the quarries. Suddenly, the ironmasters responsible began to realise that they were watching the growth of a new town, Millom, and so Holborn Hill Station became Millom Station.

The ready supply of high-grade iron ore deposits from the Hodbarrow Mine, south of Millom, fuelled the West Cumbrian and Barrow iron, steel and shipbuilding industries and the massive Park Mine complex between Barrow and Askam, while to a lesser extent the Lindal mines fed Barrow.

Millom iron mining sculpture by Humphrey Bolton. The town's ironworks closed in 1968. Hodbarrow is now the largest coastal lagoon in the North West of England.

Built in 1890, this 0-4-0 Hodbarrow crane tank, Snipey, is well-known to railway enthusiasts. Railway memorabilia and artefacts are displayed, including lamps and signals, the layouts of track and points, at the Millom Discovery Centre.

CHAPTER 7

Airships: Barrow's Involvement in the Aircraft Industry

The British Admiralty had been monitoring the German Count Ferdinand von Zeppelin's achievements in building the *LZI,* the first airship, at the turn of the century, and they were keen to create something similar for the Royal Navy. Vickers Ltd was asked by the Admiralty to submit a price for the building of a rigid airship of the Zeppelin type (the term Zeppelin came to refer to all rigid airships).

Vickers advised that it could construct the ship, HMA *No 1/R1,* (which became commonly known as the *Mayfly*), for £28,000 in return for a 10-year monopoly on airship construction. The contract was awarded to Vickers on 7 May 1909, although the 10-year clause was refused. In public records the *Mayfly* is designated 'HMA *Hermione*', because the naval contingent at Barrow was attached to HMS *Hermione*, a cruiser moored locally, which was preparing to act as *Mayfly's* tender.

***Airship News*, 28 August 1909**:

Considerable progress is being made in connection with the huge shed which Messrs. Vickers, Sons and Maxim are having built on the Cavendish Dock at Barrow to accommodate the dirigible, on Zeppelin lines, which is in course of construction for the Admiralty.

(Above) *'Won't Fly'*: Mayfly *emerging from her floating hangar (1911).*

(Below) Mayfly *collapsed (1911). The ship was designed to carry a crew of 20 in comfort.*

During the time of construction and testing of the *Mayfly*, the constructional shed along the side of the site at Cavendish Dock (the Naval Construction Yard) was affixed on pilings above the dock wall, and contrary to the Zeppelin company technique, it was not free-floating. After two years in her hangar, in 1911 *Mayfly* finally emerged. But she never flew. Battered by a 40-knot wind, she survived, yet it was found that her lifting power – which requires great experience to calculate – was insufficient. The ship was put back in her hangar and modified.

On 24 September 1911, with men and locomotives standing by, the airship was launched once again, only to be caught by a gust of wind which broke the back of the ship and crumpled it into a sorry wreck. A court of inquiry concluded that the blame for the incident could not be attributed to any individual. Commander Masterman, Officer Commanding, Naval Airship Section, is reported as stating, unofficially, that '*Mayfly* was pulled in half by the handling party when someone forgot to release the lines that tethered the bows of the ship'.

Mayfly was the subject of much negative publicity and called a waste of taxpayers' money. Winston Churchill, who was First Lord of the Admiralty at the time, made the following House of Commons statement on 26 March 1913:

> Altogether, compared with other navies, the British aeroplane service has started very well ... I have a less satisfactory account to give of airships. Naval airship developments were retarded by various causes. The mishap which destroyed the May-fly, or the Won't Fly, as it would be more accurate to call it, at Barrow, was a very serious set-back to the development of Admiralty policy in airships.

Vickers had disbanded its airship department after the Government failed to keep it supplied with work following the *Mayfly* project. A new department was constituted in April 1913, which re-assembled its original design team.

Walney Airship Sheds

Work commenced on the new Vickers hangar, Walney Airship Sheds, off Mill Lane in late 1913. It was initially built to erect two of the largest airships, so that they could be built side by side, from parts made elsewhere. Some of the airships being built at the time were portable and

Mayfly's hangar: The original Cavendish Dock constructional shed.

could be taken apart and loaded into ships or road transport for dispatch to other airship bases. Airships constructed within these sheds included *R9*, *R23*, *R26* and *R34*.

When the First World War broke out, *R9* was nearly complete. Work on *R9* continued during the first months of the war, until more concerns were expressed at the Admiralty; and on 12 March 1915 Winston Churchill cancelled the order for the ship. The reason given for this decision was that, as the war was expected to finish in 1915, the vessel would not be operational in time and thus was a waste of valuable resources. However, the war continued, and work resumed when the order was re-instated in June 1915. Final construction began in the autumn, but there were delays in obtaining flax to make nets for the gasbags and linen from Ireland when the Easter Rising broke out, and the ship was not completed until 28 June 1916.

The inside measurements of the Walney airship shed were a staggering 540 feet (165m) long, 150 feet (46m) wide, and 98 feet (30m) high. At each end of the roof were turrets, access to each provided by a staircase from the ground and a catwalk running the full length of the roof. The turrets acted as vantage points to enable airships to be safely guided in and out of the shed. At the side of the huge shed was a series of huts which accommodated up to 200 men who were required for numerous jobs but mainly for handling the huge airships in and out of the shed. A gasbag

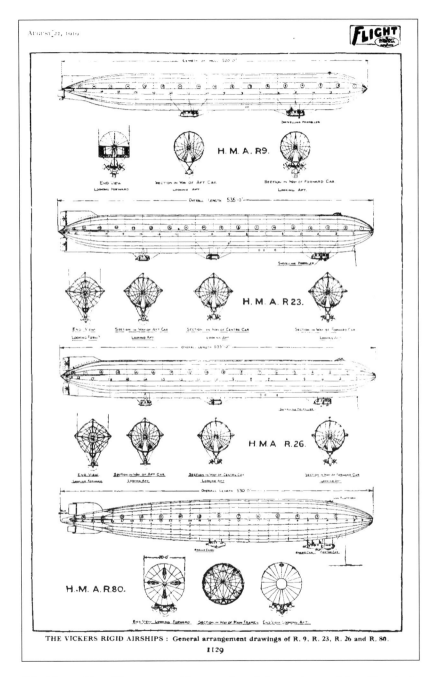

R9: Most of her life was spent in experimental mooring and handling tests, as she was still classed as an experimental ship. She provided pilots with valuable experience of handling a rigid airship and the use of mooring masts, which would evolve into a unique method of mooring airships.

R80, the final airship to be built at the site, emerging from the Walney Island shed.

factory with 100 employees was also set up beside the construction shed.

In 1917, in order to meet contractual obligations to build the *R37*, an airship too large to be constructed in the Walney shed, Vickers decided to build larger sheds at Flookburgh near Cark, south Lakeland. Work on the sheds began but in 1917 the work was halted, due to a nationwide shortage of steel. Vickers was unable to honour its contract, and it was transferred to another company.

Work continued at Walney and, apart from a small airship made for Japan, the *R80* was the last airship to be built. On 19 July 1920, the *R80* emerged from her shed for her first flight. The ship was damaged on the trial flight as the ship had not been properly ballasted, and the lifting gas superheated, causing the ship to rise too fast. The result was extensive buckling of the framework. The ship was returned to her shed and repairs commenced, taking until January 1921. Then, after further test flights, the airship flew to the airship station at Howden, East Yorkshire in February, where it was used for crew training, including the training of US personnel who would be taking charge of *R38*, the world's largest airship, which made its first flight on 23 June 1921.

After the outbreak of the First World War, the German military made extensive use of Zeppelins as bombers and scouts. They prevented British ships from approaching Germany, spotted sites where the British were laying mines and later aided the destruction of those mines. There were posters all over Barrow shipyard telling staff what to do in case of aerial bombardment and there were light restrictions on shops – with hefty fines for staying open too late. The parts of at least one First World War Zeppelin

Artist's impression of the proposed shed on Airship Shed Road, Walney, now West Shore Road, off Mill Lane. (By kind permission)

The R80, a British airship, was launched on 19 July 1920 and was the first fully streamlined airship design to be built in Britain.

were brought to Barrow's shipyard for the attention of technicians who wanted to unlock its secrets.

By mid-1917, the Zeppelin's role in attacking Britain had been largely superseded by aeroplanes and in particular the new breed of bomber known as the Gotha.

Threat from the skies: There was a very great fear of Zeppelin attacks during the war, but this fancy dress entry in a Millom carnival attempted to make a joke of it. (By kind permission)

CHAPTER 8

Vessels Built in Barrow Before and During the First World War

James Postlethwaite was the second to last schooner built in Barrow by William Ashburner and Son, and named after James Postlethwaite of Gleaston, Barrow. Launched in 1881, she was in Hamburg on the day that Britain entered the war. The Germans cut down her masts, converting her into a barge, and she was used to carry ammunition on the Elbe. Her crew was imprisoned, first in Hamburg and then transferred to Ruhleben internment camp on a racecourse at Spandau, near Berlin. She made her last visit to Barrow in 1952.

Britain and Germany entered into a dreadnought-building race from 1906; this competition is now seen as one of the causes of the First World War. Dreadnoughts were a new class of battleship designed with an 'all-big-gun' armament scheme, an unprecedented number of heavy-calibre guns, and steam turbine propulsion. Successive designs increased rapidly in size and made use of improvements in armament, armour, and propulsion.

In 1906, Britain launched the world's first dreadnought, HMS *Dreadnought*, which was built in Portsmouth. SMS *Von der Tann* (laid down in 1908, launched in 1909 and commissioned in 1910) was the first battlecruiser built for the German Kaiserliche Marine, as well as German's first major turbine-powered warship. (N.B. Commissioning marks the

Wendy Taylor's sculpture, 'Spirit of Barrow' features the names of some of the foremost vessels built in Barrow. It traces shipbuilding from the days of the Barrow Shipbuilding Company up to Trident. (Taken by the author, 2013.)

The James Postlethwaite.

occasion when a vessel is accepted into active service.) At the time of her construction, *Von der Tann* was the fastest dreadnought-type warship afloat – she could cross the North Sea in one night. She was present at the Battle of Jutland, where she destroyed British battlecruiser HMS *Indefatigable*. Only two of the *Indefatigable* crew of 1,019 survived.

HMS Calcutta at anchor.

A-Z of Ships Built in Barrow

Key to the information on vessels given below:
* Barrow built: Confirmed by the Dock Museum, Barrow
** Barrow built: Confirmed by Dock Museum and listed on the Dock Museum selection monument)

HMS *Calcutta**

HMS *Calcutta*, a C-class light cruiser, was built for the Royal Navy and named after the Indian city of Calcutta. Launched in July 1918, she was commissioned too late to see action in the First World War, but was converted into an anti-aircraft cruiser in 1939 and deployed in the Mediterranean. *Calcutta* was sunk on 1 June 1941 by Luftwaffe Junkers 88 bombers 190 km off Alexandria, Egypt.

HMCS *Canada* *

Commissioned in 1915, HMCS *Canada* served on the Atlantic coast. On 6 December 1917, she was one of the ships anchored at HMC Dockyard in Halifax Harbour during the Halifax Explosion. HMCS *Canada* was decommissioned from the Royal Canadian Navy in November 1919 and she resumed her former civilian fisheries patrol duties as CGS *Canada*.

HMCS Canada *(front) moored with the cruiser HMS* Sentinel *in Barrow, 1904.*

HMS *Dartmouth***

HMS *Dartmouth* was launched in October 1911. On the outbreak of the war, she was stationed in the East Indies and in October 1914, she captured the German tug *Adjutant*. In January 1915, *Dartmouth* was reassigned to the 2nd Light Cruiser Squadron of the Grand Fleet, but was then detached to operate in the South Atlantic in the search for the commerce raider SMS *Karlsruhe*.

In February 1915, *Dartmouth* was operating off the Dardanelles in support of the Allied landings at Gallipoli. In May 1915, she was

HMS Dartmouth: *Commissioned at Devonport for Atlantic Fleet and attached to 3rd Battle Squadron during 1912-13.*

HMS Doris *was decommissioned and scrapped in 1919.*

reassigned to the 8th Light Cruiser Squadron at Brindisi, and took part in the Battle of the Otranto Straits on the night of 14 May. She was later involved in the Battle off Durazzo, with her sister ship, HMS *Weymouth*. On 15 May 1917, she was damaged by a torpedo from *U-25*. She was scrapped in 1930.

HMS *Doris**

HMS *Doris*, an *Eclipse*-class cruiser, was built for the Royal Navy and launched in March 1896. When the war began, she was serving with the 11th Cruiser Squadron of the Home Fleet. On 5 August 1914, she captured a German merchant ship.

TS (Training Ship) *Dufferin***

TS (Training Ship) *Dufferin* was built to serve in British India. She was launched in September 1904.

HMS *Emperor of India* *

HMS *Emperor of India* was an Iron Duke-class battleship built for the Royal Navy, launched in November 1913 and commissioned in November 1914. Upon commissioning, *Emperor of India* joined the First Battle Squadron of the Grand Fleet, based at Scapa Flow, at that time the main base of the battle fleet in time of war. She later joined the Fourth Battle Squadron and was flagship of Rear-Admiral A.L. Duff.

She was being refitted in 1916, at the time of the Battle of Jutland. During Jutland, she was replaced as Admiral Duff's flagship by *Superb*. In 1917, *Emperor of India* replaced her sister ship *Marlborough* as second

Emperor of India *was present at the surrender of the German High Seas Fleet.*

flagship of the 1st Battle Squadron. *Emperor of India* was present at the surrender of the German High Seas Fleet in November 1918. She survived the post-war cuts to the Royal Navy and joined the Mediterranean Fleet in 1919. She was decommissioned in 1929 and sunk as a target ship on 1 September 1931. The following year she was raised and scrapped.

HMS *Erin* **

HMS *Erin* was a dreadnought battleship of the Royal Navy, originally built in response to an order placed by the Ottoman Government and intended to be called *Resadiye*. In 1914, when the First World War broke out, the ship was nearly complete and, on the orders of Winston Churchill, the First Lord of the Admiralty, she was seized for use by the Royal Navy. She was present at the Battle of Jutland and sold for scrap in 1922. Jutland is considered to be the only major naval battle of the First World War. It was an inconclusive battle which continues to generate debate today, as

Launch into Walney Channel: Erin, *3rd September 1913. The ship is flying the Turkish flag.*

Germany won the tactical victory, but the British claimed the more important strategic success.

HMS *Euryalus* **
HMS *Euryalus* was a Cressy-class armoured cruiser of the Royal Navy and launched in May 1901. Though the class was already obsolete by the outbreak of the First World War, due to rapid advances in naval architecture, the *Euryalus* and her sisters, *Aboukir*, *Bacchante*, *Hogue* and *Cressy*, were assigned to patrol the Broad Fourteens of the North Sea (see HMS *Hogue* listing).

As a result of the sinking of the *Hogue* and *Cressy*, the *Euryalus* and *Bacchante* were withdrawn from the North Sea and employed on the Western Channel patrol instead. *Euryalus* assisted the landings at Cape Helles, the rocky headland at the south-westernmost tip of the Gallipoli peninsula. From mid-December 1915, Admiral Sir Rosslyn Wemyss organised and commanded from *Euryalus* the evacuation of Gallipoli.

Wemyss also used *Euryalus* in his 1916-17 diplomatic and naval campaign in the Middle East, supporting the Arab Revolt against the

Launch of HMS Euryalus.

Turks, exploiting the fact that the Arabs were impressed by the ship's four funnels, which they perceived as a sign of great power. *Euryalus* continued as flagship of the East Indies Fleet until 1919, and was scrapped in 1920.

HMS *King Alfred* *

HMS *King Alfred* was launched in October 1901. This Drake-class cruiser built for the Royal Navy was scrapped in 1920. In January 1918, she and *Leviathan* escorted US troop convoys across the Atlantic.

HMS King Alfred *under construction.*

Eclipse-class cruiser HMS Juno.

HMS *Juno* *

HMS *Juno* was an Eclipse-class cruiser built for the Royal Navy. She was launched in November 1895 and scrapped in 1920. In 1912 and 1913, she acted as a parent ship of two of the torpedo-boat destroyer flotillas at Harwich, Essex.

*Katori**

Katori, a pre-dreadnought battleship, was built for the Imperial Japanese Navy and launched in 1905. She was scrapped in 1924.

Kongo *

Kongo, the first battlecruiser of the Kongo-class (among the most heavily armed ships in any navy when first built, with 14-inch guns), was made for the Imperial Japanese Navy. She was laid down in 1911 at Barrow and

Kongo: *Launched into Walney Channel in 1912. (Courtesy of Grace's Guide)*

launched into Walney Channel in 1912, then transferred to the dockyards of Portsmouth. *Kongo* was completed and commissioned into the Japanese Navy in August 1913, and patrolled off the Chinese coast during the First World War.

She fought in a large number of major naval actions of the War in the Pacific during the Second World War, before she was torpedoed and sunk by the submarine USS *Sealion*, while crossing the Formosa Strait on 21 November 1944.

HMS *Hogue* **

HMS *Hogue* was a Cressy-class armoured cruiser in the Royal Navy, launched in 1900 by Lady Muncaster, wife of the 5th Baron Muncaster, Josslyn Francis Pennington of Muncaster Castle, West Cumbria. Shortly after the outbreak of war, *Hogue* was assigned to the 7th Cruiser Squadron, and tasked with patrolling the Broad Fourteens of the North Sea, in support

The launch of HMS Hogue.

of a force of destroyers and submarines based at Harwich, Essex. This force blocked the eastern end of the Channel from German warships attempting to attack the supply route between England and France.

At 7am on 22 September 1914, *Hogue* was struck by two torpedoes from *U-9* (commanded by Otto Weddigen), as she attempted to rescue survivors from her sister ship, *Aboukir*. She sank within 15 minutes.

HMS *Liverpool* **

HMS *Liverpool*, a 4,800 ton Town-class light cruiser of the Royal Navy, was launched in October 1910. She served in home waters and was subordinated to the Home Fleet from 1909 and through the initial stages of the war. During the war, *Liverpool* fought in the Battle of Heligoland Bight, operated off the coast of West Africa and served in the Adriatic and Aegean. She was notably involved in the rescue of the crew of *Audacious* on 27 October 1914 and attempted to tow the ship to port before the battleship capsized and exploded. She was scrapped in 1921.

Otto Weddigen was awarded Prussia's highest military order, the Pour le Mérite, *for the sinking of HMS Hawke.*

On 27 October 1914 HMS Audacious *sank in Loch Swilly, near Tory Island, when the battleship hit a mine laid by the SMS* Berlin. *HMS* Liverpool *(left) and HMS* Fury *attempt to tow the stricken ship. This photograph was taken from RMS* Olympic, *a sister ship of the* Titanic.

Mikasa *is now a museum ship in Yokosuka, Japan.*

Mikasa**

The pre-dreadnought battleship *Mikasa* was launched at Barrow in 1900, when Japanese naval officials and sailors would have been a relatively common sight in the town.

Mikasa became the flagship of the Japanese fleet in Japan's war with Russia from 1904 to 1905. At the end of the war, the American forces dismantled the ship's armaments and it was not until 1955 that a drive to restore the ship to her former glory was initiated by the *Japan Times*, which ran a fundraising campaign. The refurbishment was completed in 1961 and since then she has been a museum ship in Yokosuka, Japan.

HMS *Natal* **

HMS *Natal* was a Duke of Edinburgh-class armoured cruiser built for the Royal Navy and launched in March 1907. In 1915, she was destroyed by an internal explosion at Cromarty, Scotland, thought to be due to faulty cordite. Most of her wreck was slowly salvaged over the decades, until the remnants were demolished in the 1970s so that they were no longer a hazard to navigation.

HMS Natal, *1905-1915.*

HMS *Niobe*/HMCS *Niobe* *

HMS *Niobe*/HMCS *Niobe* was launched in February 1897. This Diadem-class cruiser built for the Royal Navy/Royal Canadian Navy was scrapped in 1922. In 1914, *Niobe* sailed on her first wartime operational mission to escort the transport *Canada*, carrying The Royal Canadian Regiment to garrison duty in Bermuda. She joined a fruitless search for a reported German surface raider in the straits of Belle Isle, a waterway in eastern Canada. In September 1915, *Niobe* returned to Halifax, Canada, where she was used as a depot ship for the rest of the war.

HMS *Penelope**

HMS *Penelope* was an Arethusa-class light cruiser of the Royal Navy launched in August 1914. Unlike her sisters, she carried an extra 4-inch anti-aircraft gun in place of two 3-inch anti-aircraft guns. In April 1916, she was damaged by torpedo from *U-29* off the Norfolk coast. She was scrapped in 1924.

HMS *Phaeton* *

HMS *Phaeton* was launched in February 1915 and was present at the Battle of Jutland. She was scrapped in 1923.

HMS *Powerful**

HMS *Powerful*, a Powerful-class cruiser, was built for the Royal Navy and launched in July 1895.

HMS Powerful *was launched in 1895.*

HMS *Princess Royal***

HMS *Princess Royal,* launched in October 1911 and commissioned in 1912, was the second of two Lion-class battlecruisers built for the Royal Navy before the war. Designed in response to the Moltke-class battlecruisers of the German Navy, the ships significantly improved on the speed, armament and armour of the preceding *Indefatigable* class.

Princess Royal served in the Battle of Heligoland Bight a month after the war began. She was then sent to the Caribbean to prevent the German East Asia Squadron from using the Panama Canal. After the East Asia Squadron was sunk at the Battle of the Falkland Islands in December 1914, *Princess Royal* rejoined the 1st Battlecruiser Squadron. During the Battle

HMS Princess Royal.

of Dogger Bank, *Princess Royal* scored few hits, although one crippled the German armoured cruiser *Blücher*. Shortly afterwards, she became the flagship of the 1st Battlecruiser Squadron, under the command of Rear-Admiral Osmond Brock.

Princess Royal was damaged during the Battle of Jutland and required repairs. Apart from providing distant support during the Second Battle of Heligoland Bight in 1917, the ship spent the rest of the war on uneventful patrols of the North Sea. *Princess Royal* was scrapped in 1922.

HMS *Revenge***
HMS *Revenge* was a Revenge-class battleship built for the Royal Navy. She was launched in May 1915 and was present at the Battle of Jutland, where she fired 102-inch x 15-inch shells and received no damage. She was scrapped in 1948.

Ryurik **
The Russian cruiser *Ryurik* was an armoured cruiser built for the Imperial Russian Navy. She was launched in November 1906 and scrapped in 1930. There are three Russian graves towards the low part of Barrow Cemetery, including that of Dmitry Vavelevich Tyrinz, Chief Inspector of the Artillery Unit, who died in Barrow in 1915. He may have been in Barrow to examine the latest armaments. Mining Engineer N.I. Dobronravov died in

Ryurik: *The Russian Navy was an unusual customer for a British shipyard.*

the town in 1907, after an illness, and Andrei Kopitin, a stoker on board the cruiser *Bogatyr,* died of heart disease in Barrow in 1906, aged 24.

Sao Paulo **

Sao Paulo, a Minas Geraes-class battleship, was built for the Brazilian Navy and launched in 1909. She sank during adverse weather in 1951.

HMS *Triumph* *

HMS *Triumph* was the second of the two Swiftsure-class pre-dreadnought battleships of the Royal Navy. Purchased from Chile before completion, she was initially assigned to the Home Fleet and Channel Fleets, before being transferred to the Mediterranean Fleet in 1909 and to the China Station in 1913. *Triumph* participated in the hunt for the German East Asia Squadron of German Admiral Maximilian Graf von Spee, and in the campaign against the German colony at Tsingtao, China early in the war.

HMS Triumph *nearing completion in 1904.*

The ship was transferred to the Mediterranean in early 1915 to participate in the Dardanelles Campaign against the Ottoman Empire. She was torpedoed and sunk off Gaba Tepe, Gallipoli, by *U-21* on 25 May 1915. Three officers and 75 enlisted men died during her sinking.

HMS Vanguard *afloat after being launched. Guests at the launch included the ship's sponsor, Mrs McKenna, the wife of the First Lord of the Admiralty.*

HMS Vanguard: *The ship's bell from* Vanguard, *which is held in the Barrow Dock Museum. The date on the bell, March 1910, represents the date of the ship's commissioning. (Taken by the author, 2013).*

HMS *Vanguard* **

HMS *Vanguard* was a St Vincent-class battleship built for the Royal Navy. She was ordered in 1908, launched in 1909 and in 1910 commissioned at Devonport in the first division of the Home Fleet. On the outbreak of war, *Vanguard* joined the First Battle Squadron at Scapa Flow, and fought in the Battle of Jutland as part of the Fourth Battle Squadron. Just before midnight on 9 July 1917 at Scapa Flow, *Vanguard* suffered an explosion. She sank almost instantly, with the loss of 804 men; there were only two survivors.

The site of her wreck is now designated as a controlled site under the Protection of Military Remains Act. In terms of loss of life, the destruction of the *Vanguard* remains the most catastrophic accidental explosion in the history of the UK, and one of the worst accidental losses of the Royal Navy. One of the victims was Petty Officer Alfred Thomson of Hindpool Road, Barrow. He had been inspired to join the Royal Navy, in 1903, aged 16, by the building of the *Mikasa* in the local shipyard.

HMS *Vengeance* *

HMS *Vengeance* was launched in 1899. She was the first Royal Naval ship to be built, engineered, armoured and supplied with her heavy gun mountings by one firm. On the outbreak of war, *Vengeance* was assigned to the 8th Battle Squadron, Channel Fleet, for patrol duties in the English Channel and Atlantic, transferring to the 7th Battle Squadron in August 1914 to relieve battleship *Prince George* as flagship.

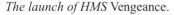

The launch of HMS Vengeance.

She covered the landing of the Plymouth Marine Battalion at Ostend, Belgium on 25 August 1914. In November 1914, she transferred to West Africa, then to Egypt, and later moved on to the Cape Verde-Canary Islands Station. *Vengeance* arrived at the Dardanelles in February 1915. She participated in the opening bombardment of the Ottoman Turkish entrance forts on 18 February and 19 February 1915, suffering some damage to her masts and rigging. She also took part in the main attack on the Narrows forts on 18 March 1915, supporting the main landings at Cape Helles in the Morto Bay area on 25 April 1915 and the ground troops during the Turkish attack on Allied positions at Anzac Cove on 19 May 1915.

By July 1915, *Vengeance* had boiler defects which prevented her from continuing combat operations and she was subsequently under refit at Devonport until December 1915. *Vengeance* left for a deployment to the Cape and East Africa. In 1917, she returned to the UK, where she became an ammunition store ship, and was scrapped in 1921.

Ying Swei **

Ying Swei, a Chao Ho-class cruiser, was built for the Chinese Navy and launched in December 1911. She was sunk in the Second Sino-Japanese War in 1937.

Submarines

The German Navy's most formidable weapon was the U-boat, a submarine far more sophisticated than those built by any other nation at the time. The typical U-boat was 214 feet long, carried 35 men and 12 torpedoes, and could travel underwater for two hours at a time. U-boats tried to target unarmed merchant ships and trawlers. *U-35* ended up being the most successful U-boat participating in the First World War: it sank 224 vessels (excluding warships) during 17 patrols from November 1914 and remained in action to the very last point in the conflict, when she was surrendered and broken up at Blyth, Northumberland.

British submarines had an inauspicious start in World War One and their development in the years leading up to the war was fraught with many problems. However, together with the natural design developments which occurred alongside certain technical developments, by 1918 the submarine represented a formidable weapon of war for the Royal Navy.

A-Z of Submarines Built in Barrow

Abdül Hamid *

The Nordenfelt-class *Abdül Hamid* was an early steam powered submarine built in 1886. She was bought and put in service by the Ottoman Navy and named after Sultan Abdül Hamid II. She was also the first submarine in the world to fire a live torpedo underwater. The *Abdül Hamid* was pulled from active service in 1910, because her speed and (submerged) range was limited at best.

The Abdül Hamid.

HMS *A1***

HMS *A1*, A-class, was built for the Royal Navy and launched in July 1902. She became the Royal Navy's first submarine casualty, being rammed and sunk whilst on exercise in the Eastern Solent on 18 March 1904 by the mail steamer *Berwick Castle*. She sank in only 39 feet of water, with the loss of all hands, including Lieutenant Loftus Charles Ogilvy Mansergh, aged 37, who served with The Royal Warwickshire Regiment.

A1 was recovered and employed for training and experimental work in anti-submarine warfare. In 1911, she was rendered unfit for service after an explosion the previous year and was subsequently engaged in unmanned trials. While operating under automatic pilot as a submerged target she was lost off Selsey Bill, West Sussex. A local fisherman snagged the wreck by chance in 1989 and his contact with diver Martin Woodward led to its identification. The vessel was purchased by Mr Woodward from the Ministry of Defence in 1994 and he recovered the bronze conning

The ill-fated A1 *sank twice.*

tower hatch, in an attempt to make the wreck less attractive to trophy-hunting divers. The submarine lies at a depth of 11-12 metres.

HMS *A2* **

HMS *A2* was built for the Royal Navy and launched in April 1903. She was scrapped in January 1920. During the First World War, *A2* served on harbour service at Portsmouth.

HMS *A3* **

HMS *A3* was built for the Royal Navy and launched in July 1904. On 2 February 1912, she was accidentally rammed whilst surfacing by the submarine tender *Hazard* off the Isle of Wight and sank with the loss of all hands on board.

A3 *sank in 1912, off the coast of the Isle of Wight.*

HMS *A4* **

HMS *A4* was built for the Royal Navy and launched in July 1904. During the First World War, she was used for training at Portsmouth. She was scrapped in January 1920.

HMS *A5* **

HMS *A5* was built for the Royal Navy and launched in February 1905. She was scrapped in 1920.

HMS *A7* **

HMS *A7* was built for the Royal Navy and laid down in February 1903. On 16 January 1914, she was exercising in Whitsands Bay, Cornwall when she dived to carry out a mock attack on her escorts and failed to resurface. Her crew of 11 officers and men were lost.

HMS A7 *was laid down in 1903.*

HMS *A11* **

HMS *A11* was built for the Royal Navy and launched in March 1905. She was scrapped in May 1920.

HMAS *AE1* **

HMAS *AE1* was built for the Royal Australian Navy and launched in May 1913. She was lost at sea on 14 September 1914, with the loss of 35 crew members (15 Australians and 20 Britons), during the campaign to seize the colony of German New Guinea, now Papua New Guinea. *AE1*, captained by Liverpool man Thomas Besant, has never been found but one theory is that the steering jammed, taking the vessel on to a reef. It was believed to have had eight unstable torpedoes on board, but has evaded all endeavours to locate it.

Descendants of the *AE1*'s crew have for years tried to find the boat and believe the vessel can be located, solving one of Australia's last maritime mysteries. An *AE1* seaman's diary, written six months before she was lost, is available online (at *navyhistory.org.au*).

HMAS *AE2* **

HMAS *AE2* was built for the Royal Australian Navy and launched in June 1913. She was scuttled on 29 April 1915.

HMAS AE2 *in Sydney.*

C-class Submarines

Some 38 C-class subs were built in Barrow for the Royal Navy before the First World War.

HMS *E4* **

HMS *E4* was built for the Royal Navy and launched in February 1912. On 24 September 1915, *E4* was attacked by the German airship *SL3*. On 15 August 1916, she collided with sister ship *E41* during exercises off Harwich, Essex. Both ships sank.

Underway in the Hollands

Holland 1 **

Holland 1 was the first submarine commissioned by the Royal Navy. In order to keep her construction secret, she was assembled in a building labelled 'Yacht Shed', and parts fabricated in the general yard were marked for 'pontoon no 1'. She was launched in October 1901 – the launch too was carried out in great secrecy – and dived for the first time (in an enclosed basin) in March 1902. Sea trials began in April 1902. In September 1902, she arrived at Portsmouth.

In October 1904, she sailed from Portsmouth to attack a Russian fleet which had mistakenly sunk a number of British fishing vessels in the North Sea in the Dogger Bank incident. The boats were recalled before any attack could take place. *Holland 1* was decommissioned and sold in 1913, by which time she was considered so obsolete that she was sold with all fittings intact and the only requirement made of the purchaser was that the torpedo tube be put out of action. *Holland 1* is preserved at the Royal Navy Submarine Museum in Gosport, Hampshire.

Holland 1: *Considered obsolete by 1913.*

A painting of the interior of Holland I *by the artist Geoff Hunt. (By kind permission)*

Holland I was originally developed by a former monk and financed by Irish revolutionaries. John Philip Holland (1841–1914) was born in County Clare, where he joined a religious order in Cork at the age of 17. Maritime ideas distracted him from a spiritual calling, however, and he began to draw sketches of submersible boats. He left the order to join the exodus to America. In 1873, he submitted his drawings to the American Navy, and they were rejected.

However, the American branch of the Irish patriots, the Fenian Society, heard about Holland's work and gave him $6,000 to build two submarines, which they planned to use against the Royal Navy. The Fenian Brotherhood was founded in New York, by veterans of the 1848 Irish uprising, and intended to raise funds for the recruitment and training of exiles to fight for Irish independence.

With extra funds from the Fenian Brotherhood, Irish engineer John Philip Holland was able to give up his teaching job and concentrate on his experiments.

The public launch of Holland 2.

Holland 2 *

Holland 2, Holland-class, was the first Royal Navy submarine not to be given a secret launch. She was commissioned in August 1902 and she set the depth record for the British *Holland*-class, by accidentally diving to 78 feet. In December 1902, she sustained some minor damage after a current took her off course and she accidentally surfaced directly underneath a brigantine.

Holland 4 *

Holland 4, Holland-class, was built for the Royal Navy and laid down in 1902. She foundered on 3 September 1912, but was salvaged and used as a gunnery target on 17 October 1914.

Gunnery target: Holland 4.

Holland 5 *

Holland 5, Holland-class, carried one of the earliest periscopes. She sank whilst under tow to the scrapyard in 1912, possibly caused by her torpedo hatch being left open.

Holland 6 *

What was intended as *Holland 6* emerged as HMS *A1*. Captain Reginald Bacon, the first inspecting captain of submarines, had decided that the *Holland* class submarines were too small to be of any practical value.

HMS *K4* **

HMS *K4* was built for the Royal Navy and laid down in 1915. *K4* was sunk on 31 January 1918 during exercises with the 13th submarine flotilla.

Laid down in 1915, HMS K4 *ran aground on Walney Island in January 1917.*

L-class Submarines **

Some 25 L-class submarines were built for the Royal Navy in Barrow between 1917 and 1919.

HMS *M1* **

HMS *M1* was built for the Royal Navy and launched in July 1917. She was fitted with a 12-inch gun able to hit targets positioned over 20 miles

HMS M1: *Note the distinctive camouflage pattern and the massive 12-inch deck gun.*

away. She was sunk during an exercise off the Devon coast, after colliding with Swedish Collier SS *Vidar*. All crew members were lost.

HMS *M2* **

HMS *M2*, the world's first underwater aircraft carrier, was built for the Royal Navy and laid down in 1916. All 60 crew members, including two airmen, were killed when *M2* sank in 1932. It is believed that disaster

HMS M2 was an experimental submarine designed to launch aeroplanes.

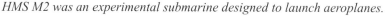

struck 3 miles off Lyme Bay, Dorset when the hangar door opened too early and the vessel was still submerged. Only two bodies were ever recovered and now the British Sub-Aqua Club at Portsmouth keeps watch on the protected site and designated war grave. The hangar door is still open.

HMS *R7* **

HMS *R7* was built for the Royal Navy and launched in May 1918. HMS *R8*, built for the Royal Navy, was launched in June 1918. They were launched too late to see any combat in the First World War.

A-Z of Passenger Ferry/Seaplane Carriers built in Barrow

HMS *Ben-my-Chree* *

HMS *Ben-my-Chree*, a passenger ferry/seaplane carrier, was built for the Isle of Man Steam Packet and launched in 1908. She was sunk on 11 January 1917 by shore-based Turkish artillery fire.

Oil Tankers Built in Barrow: *Marinula/Santa Margherita/Trigonia* *

Marinula/Santa Margherita/Trigonia was an oil tanker built for Eagle Oil and launched in 1916. She was scrapped in 1951.

HMS Ben-my-Chree, *launched in 1908.*

A-Z of Cargo Ships and Other Vessels Built in Barrow

Affonso Penna *
Affonso Penna, floating dry dock class, was built for the Brazilian Government. She was launched in June 1910.

Anglia *
Anglia, a cable ship, was built for the Telegraph Construction and Maintenance Company and launched in June 1898.

Duke of Connaught *
Duke of Connaught, floating dry dock class, was built for the Canadian arm of Vickers in Montreal and launched in 1912.

HMCS Earl Grey *
HMCS *Earl Grey*, ice breaker class, was built for the Canadian Government and launched in June 1909.

HMS Exmouth *
HMS *Exmouth*/HMS *Worcester*, school ship class, was built for the Metropolitan Asylums Board and launched in April 1905. She became accommodation for the Royal Navy at the Scapa Flow naval base, in the south of the Orkney Islands, in 1914.

Oruba I *
Oruba I was a passenger liner built for the Pacific Steam Navigation Company and launched in 1889. In late 1914, Churchill came up with the idea of disguising merchant ships as capital ships to fool the Germans. She was purchased by the British Admiralty in 1914 and modified to represent the super-dreadnought battleship HMS *Orion*. She was scuttled at Mudros Harbour in Lemnos, Greece as a breakwater in 1915.

The Walney Island Wrecks, 1914-1918
The 'Back of Wanna' has ever been a terror to seamen, and will remain so. Many a gallant ship has gone to pieces there. In 1914, British steamship *Vedra* (built in 1893 by Laing James & Sons Ltd), carrying benzene, ran aground on 7 December and exploded on 8 December, with the loss of 31 lives and leaving only one survivor. On 7 February 1918, the steamship *Limesfield* (built in 1916 by Lytham Shipbuilding, Lancashire), while on a voyage from Belfast to Preston with a cargo of waste, was sunk by *UB-57*, or possibly *U-96*, 23 miles west-north-west of Walney. There were no casualties.

CHAPTER 9

Barrow's Munitions Output

Shortage of ammunition was a serious problem for the British armed forces right from the start of the war, and by May 1915 it was threatening to undermine the whole of the British war effort. Trench warfare had become reality and artillery was the major weapon in this type of conflict.

During the war years Barrow was flooded with munitions girls, with many arriving from mill towns in Yorkshire and Lancashire. Some women travelled to work in Barrow all the way from the Isle of Man and one Manx woman, Mary Faragher, worked as a crane driver at the Vickers Naval Armaments Factory.

Women enrol at the Barrow Labour Exchange in order to obtain work in the munitions factories.

Shells piled up in the shell shop in the Barrow Yard at Vickers Ltd, pictured on 12 December 1915.

Hundreds of local girls also went to work in the Vickers shell shops. The work they did was complex, often skilled and it involved using heavy engineering machinery, such as belt-driven lathes. Workers on the production line assembled shells and great care was taken with the detonator just before weighing the shell. Eventually, the Barrow shell shops produced 6.8 million shells and 8.7 million forgings and partly completed shells.

War Work for Convalescent Soldiers
In addition to the influx of 'munitionettes', a substantial proportion of munitions workers in Barrow during the war were recuperating soldiers, who had been sent home to recover from their wounds while undertaking useful war work at the same time. Some met and married local girls, then were sent back to the Front, never to return.

Augustus Neser, of the South African Regiment, joined the Colours in South Africa in 1914, fought through the West African campaign and afterwards volunteered for overseas service, being drafted to France in 1915. He was wounded and sent to Barrow on munitions work in February 1916. That December he married a local woman, Edith Bird, who is listed on the 1911 census as a hosiery examiner from Roanhead. After rejoining his regiment, Augustus was drafted to France in August 1918. He was killed in action in October 1918 and left Edith to bring up their child alone. Pte Neser is commemorated on the Askam War Memorial and the Ireleth-with-Askam (St Peter's) Church War Memorial.

Unguarded Machinery
The following is an extract from an interview with a former wartime munitions worker, conducted by Elizabeth Roberts, the author of *Working Class Barrow and Lancaster 1890 to 1930*:

This appears to be the most likely Edith Bird who married Augustus Neser. He, of course, would have been in South Africa at the time of the Census. By kind permission.

She hadn't a hat on and of course it was a drilling machine. They're easy enough to work them drilling machines, you just drill a hole, the hole for the screw. Anyway she just happened to turn her head and her hair was loose and she caught her hair in it. The screams, it was terrible, I remember it now. She hadn't the sense ... she was too shocked to pull the lever to stop the machine ... One just ran and stopped the machine and got her out. It pulled her hair out, it pulled her scalp ... But it was through not wearing a hat. So of course they fined them and they fined them more after that because we were supposed to wear them. For practical reasons, during the war, women munition workers began to shorten their skirts.

Accidents were plentiful in the days of unguarded machinery and explosions were a constant risk. The National Filling Factory No. 1 in Barnbow, near Leeds lost 35 women workers in a single ammunition explosion in 1916.

The Lady Superintendent
Dorothée Aurélie Marianne Pullinger (1894–1986) was of the generation of women who grew up in the years of the militant women's suffrage campaigns. When the war broke out, she was appointed as the manager of

women newly employed by Vickers, eventually becoming responsible for over 7,000 female munitions workers. She was awarded an MBE in recognition of her war work in 1920, and later in the decade, Dorothée and her husband Edward Marshall Martin established White Service Laundries in Croydon. During World War Two, she was the only woman appointed to the Industrial Panel of the Ministry of Production.

Howitzers at Vickers

Naval guns were made in the Ordnance Department of Vickers, which turned out 11,740 vehicles for 18-pound guns alone and 30,000 tons of howitzer equipments, according to a report in *The Times* in 1919.

Businesswoman Dorothée Pullinger. In 1914, she applied to join the Institution of Automobile Engineers, but was refused on the grounds that 'the word person means a man and not a woman.'

Howitzers were particularly useful for delivering cast-iron shells filled with gunpowder or incendiary materials into the interior of fortifications. The onset of trench warfare, after the first few months of the war, greatly increased the demand for howitzers that gave a steep angle of descent. These were better suited than guns to striking targets in a vertical plane, such as trenches, with large amounts of explosive and considerably less barrel wear.

The Projectile Factory

Vickers, working on behalf of the Ministry of Munitions, was also responsible for supervising and staffing a 33-acre shell making factory at Lancaster, the Projectile Factory (erected in September 1915), and a shell filling factory at White Lund, Morecambe (National Filling Factory No 13). A filling factory was a type of munitions factory that specialised in filling various munitions, such as bombs, shells, cartridges, pyrotechnics and smoke shells. The majority of the employees at filling factories during the war were women.

A huge explosion ripped through the filling factory at White Lund on 1 October 1917, leaving 10 dead, the majority of whom had been involved in trying to quell the blaze. A letter written in the 1960s by Mrs Grisedale, a Barrovian who witnessed the explosion, gives some indication of the shock this event caused in the town where the war had already given rise to all kinds of fears and confusion. She describes her family's reaction to the blast: 'My dad came upstairs and woke us all up and said, "The

Germans are here," so we all went into the cellar.' Closer to the factory there was chaos as windows were blown out as far away as Lancaster and hundreds of Morecambe residents fled to beaches.

One farmer provided shelter for 400 frightened people, while an engine driver won the Edward Medal for his bravery in moving to safety a line of rail trucks, which were filled with live shells. Nine firemen later received the OBE and a British Empire Medal went to Mary Wilkinson, who coordinated calls from the emergency services through the telephone exchange for 24 hours without a break.

The factory was so badly wrecked by the explosion that it was out of commission for the rest of the war. The cause of the disaster was never found, though some suspected sabotage by a spy or a Zeppelin air raid. After the war, the White Lund Factory began to operate again, but disaster struck once more on 14 January 1920, when an explosion occurred while staff defused and emptied shells. Nine people were killed. The site is now home to The White Lund Industrial Estate, and on occasion unexploded shells are still discovered nearby.

Campaigner for Women War Workers

In September 1916, the secretary of the Barrow Labour Party, Bram Longstaffe, found himself facing charges of inciting a public disturbance. He had been agitating for better pay and lodgings on behalf of munitions girls brought into Barrow from Wigan to work at Vickers.

Mr Longstaffe was found guilty and sentenced to one month's imprisonment with hard labour. Upon serving his sentence, Mr Longstaffe refused his call-up and was sent to a Welsh camp as a conscientious objector. There, he refused to obey any orders he believed would aid the war effort and he was subsequently sentenced to two years' imprisonment in Wakefield Prison.

Conscientious objector and campaigner for women workers' rights, Bram Longstaffe.

His conscientious objector status did not affect his political career. After the war, Mr Longstaffe became a town councillor and served two terms as Mayor of the Borough of Barrow, from 1934 to 1936.

CHAPTER 10

Women's Wartime Work in Barrow

Before the war, the range of job opportunities for women in Barrow was very limited, and most labourers needed to work overtime in order to support their families. Women worked as hard in the home, however, as any paid worker in the mill or factory. They exerted a prodigious amount of energy hauling buckets of water for washing boilers, dolly tubs and baths; mangling clothes; scrubbing floors and doorsteps; turning flock and feather mattresses; and kneading bread dough.

The highest proportion of Barrow women in full-time work were engaged in domestic work; others were ship workers, confectioners, dressmakers and labourers in the local Jute Works, founded by James Ramsden in 1870, in an attempt to diversify Barrow's economy. In 1911, the Jute Works employed 457 women.

The Barrow-in-Furness Tramways Company system was opened to the public on 11 July 1885. The initial tram routes were Town Hall to Abbey, with short workings to White House and Hawcoat Lane; and Town Hall to Roose, with short workings to Washington Hotel. In 1904 British Electric Traction (BET) bought the company, and by 1911, electric trams were operating widely throughout the town. Routes ran from Town Hall to Ramsden Dock, with short workings to Tea House; Town Hall to Ferry Road; and a service to Walney Promenade which was extended in 1911 to Biggar Bank.

Laundry in bygone years: Everything was washed, dried and ironed, without electricity, using rudimentary gadgets like this mangle. (Taken at the Barrow Dock Museum by the author, 2013)

A good drying day in Ship Street, Barrow, c. 1910.

Gouache painting of the Barrow and Calcutta Jute Company Works, by G.H. Andrews, dated 1875. (By kind permission).

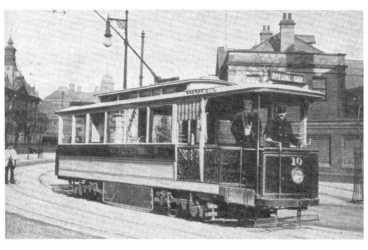

Manpower shortage: The Barrow-in-Furness Tramways Company struggled to cope in the war, taking on female workers for the first time.

The outbreak of the war restricted the expansion plans for the tram routes and the lack of men and materials put a strain on the system. In the meantime, a British Electric Traction motor bus service from Barrow Town Hall to Ulverston via Dalton commenced in 1915. During the war, women tram conductors were also employed by BET and a few later became drivers. Annie Wilkinson was one of Barrow's first lady tram drivers and it is likely she was recruited during the war.

Motorwoman: Annie Wilkinson, Barrow tram driver, dressed in her uniform. She appears to have worn the same uniform as other female staff, but with the addition of a baggy cap bearing an 'Inspector' badge.

Studio portrait of three Barrow tram conductresses, taken during the war. Note the BET 'Magnet & Wheel' cap badge on the bonnets.

Elsewhere, local women worked as teachers, replacing male staff during the war, and at Vickers as typists, timekeepers, clerks, in the wages office, in the general store and in senior-management offices. Some worked for Vickers in the Cavendish Airship Shed, where they sewed sailcloth for the outer skins of airships. Schoolchildren in the town were pressed into service knitting mufflers, gloves and balaclavas for soldiers in the trenches.

The White Feather Campaign

A simple white feather was used in a 2008 exhibition at Lancaster University to symbolise a provocative campaign led by British women during the war. The White Feather Brigade handed out white feathers to any young men seen not wearing a military uniform, whom they accused of cowardice to shame them into enlisting.

Elizabeth Walker, who created the exhibition, told the *Evening Mail* (18 September 2008):

> This would have been extremely effective in a town the size and location of Barrow, as there would have been no place to hide or avoid peer pressure from the rest of the town. This may have also caused negative feeling towards these women in the town as families of young men who were disabled, ill or refused entry to the war due to being physically weak may not have felt the unifying efforts of the local business, papers and most of all the White Feather Brigade.

Elizabeth went on to describe how her great-grandmother (also named Elizabeth Walker) was always well-dressed after she joined the local munitions factory in 1916 and enjoyed spending the extra money she had. Independent women workers, like Elizabeth's grandmother, also discovered a new-found confidence. Elizabeth added: 'The change in the social climate of the time did affect Elizabeth Walker, especially in her confidence towards social interactions with men. She wrote to and met up with Irvin Walker, her future husband.'

The Voluntary Aid Detachment

During the First World War, the Voluntary Aid Detachment (VAD) played a key role in providing field nursing services, mainly in hospitals. Barrow was too remote to receive direct casualties from the Western Front, who were sent to hospitals around the southern ports and London. There was, however, a military hospital in Cambridge Street, Barrow Island, which became a wartime convalescent hospital, accommodating men who were out of danger.

First World War recruitment poster: 'V.A.D.' by Joyce Dennys.

Other hospitals in the area, including North Lonsdale at Ulverston, may also have accommodated servicemen. The Workhouse, at Rampside Road, Barrow (erected in 1878-9), and known as the 'Big House on the Hill', served as a military hospital during the Great War.

Land Girls

The Women's Land Army (WLA) was founded in 1917. Agricultural areas, such as south Lakeland relied on Land Girls to supplement their workforce, as labourers joined up or faced conscription. By the time the WLA was established, food production had become a matter of grave national importance, as German U-Boats targeted British merchant vessels and rationing was introduced.

An armband worn by members of the Women's Land Army.

Despite the importance of the work done by the Women's Land Army, the government still felt that it was appropriate to warn Land Girls about the high standards expected of them: 'You are doing a man's work and so you are dressed rather like a man; but remember that because you wear a smock and trousers you should take care to behave like an English girl who expects chivalry and respect from everyone she meets.'

Dalton's Drink Shops

Although the licensing laws were tightened during the war, according to press reports women's drinking habits were transformed. With so many men away at the Front, many women found themselves freed from domestic restraints. They flocked to pubs, traditionally the preserve of men, and drank alcohol in greater quantities than ever before.

In *Gender, Class and Public Drinking in Britain during the First World War*, David W Gutze commented: 'Even in smaller towns like Dalton-in-Furness, women braved male hostility and entered drink shops. "You'd got to get used to it", mused a beerhouse keeper's daughter, "because it's all going then".'

CHAPTER 11

Not as Glorious as Some Would Have It

Group of soldiers of the 1st/4th Battalion, King's Own Royal Lancaster Regiment, pictured on the Somme, in 1916.

Wartime Movements of 1st/4th Battalion, King's Own Royal Lancaster Regiment

4 August 1914	Mobilised at Barrow
Winter 1914-1915	Stationed in southern England
3 May 1915	Arrived in France. Landed at Boulogne. Joined 154th Infantry Brigade, 51st Infantry Division
15 June 1915	Participated in the Battle of Festubert
7 January 1916	Joined 164th Infantry Brigade of 55th West Lancashire Division
8 August 1916	The Somme: Battle of Guillemont; Attack on Trones Wood
11 September 1916	The Somme: Battle of Ginchy; Attack on Delville Wood
27 September 1916	The Somme: Battle of Flers
28 September 1916	Attack near Mametz
23 December 1916	Raid on Cameroon Trench
9 June 1917	Raid on Ibex Trench
31 July 1917	3rd Battle of Ypres: Battle of Pilckem Ridge Attack on Wieltje
20 September 1917	3rd Battle of Ypres: Battle of the Menin Road Ridge
November 1917	Battle of Cambrai
20 November 1917	Attack near Guillemont Farm
30 November 1917	Repulse of counter-attack near Epéhy
March/April 1918	Retreat
9-11 April 1918	Battle of Estaires – First Defence of Givenchy
26 April 1918	Counter-attack on Givenchy Craters
24 August 1918	Givenchy Craters
October/November 1918	Advance to Victory
4 November 1918	Battle of the Sambre – Advance on Ath
12 December 1918	Moved to Brussels
April 1919	Returned to England

(Source: King's Own Royal Regiment Museum, Lancaster)

Widespread Casualties

It is likely that, as the months passed, many Barrovians would have come to regard initial assertions that the war would be over by Christmas 1914 – the 'Hun' rapidly beaten by the gallant British troops with minimal losses – as arrant nonsense. There had been enough casualties amongst the Regular and Reservist servicemen among the local population to dispel such thoughts.

However, these deaths had occurred in a steady trickle and people had not yet had news of more widespread casualties. This all changed with the arrival of the 1st/4th King's Own Royal Lancaster Regiment in France on 3 May 1915. At the end of the month a stray shell wiped out five members of the regiment and wounded many more.

Millom Gazette, **Friday, 4 June 1915**:

> News has been received at Barrow that the 4th King's Own Royal Lancasters, who went into the trenches in France about a week ago, have sustained casualties. One of those killed is Company Quartermaster-Sergeant Hubert W. Page of C Company, King's Own. His death, age 37, on 29th May 1915, was caused by a shell near Windy Corner, Festubert.

Hubert Page was killed in 1915, while serving with the 4th King's Own Royal Lancaster Regiment. He was, by profession, an engineering draughtsman at Vickers.

Soon after the deaths of Sergeant Page and his comrades came more bad news. On 8 June 1915, on their first foray into the trenches near Rue d'Ouvert, a shell killed 10 more local men. Corporal William Henry Milton, aged 27, was one of six Millom soldiers lost in the blast. He had worked for the Hodbarrow Mining Co and left behind a wife and son. Two of the other soldiers who alongside him were Sergeant F. Burn and Private W. M. Holmes.

Five of the Millom men died instantaneously, due to a German shell exploding in their trench. The men were buried that same night behind the trenches and a cross was put up to mark their graves.

Corporal William Milton (seated, bottom right). It is likely that this photograph was taken when he was on active service with the 4th Battalion, as he can be seen to be wearing a star on his right sleeve, denoting five years' service and he had originally enlisted in 1909.

William Milton with his wife Beatrice and son, William Donald.

'Dear Will': Postcard sent to William Milton by his wife, Beatrice Milton. (By kind permission.)

'To my Dear Husband': Birthday card dated 13 November 1914, sent by Beatrice Milton to her husband William at Slough for his twenty-seventh birthday on 15 November. William spent his birthday serving with 'H' Company, 4th Battalion, King's Own, at Upton Towers, Slough. (By kind permission.)

To the deceased men's families and friends back at home this would have been a disaster: more than 60 local men had been killed in little over a fortnight. This was a watershed moment for many people in Barrow; it was certainly a baptism of fire for the men of the Battalion. It hammered home to them just how brutal the war was going to be and warned them to prepare for more of the same.

The tragedy was also compounded by their relatives' uncertainty, in most cases, of the men's fates. Most of the men were initially posted as missing in action and their relatives clung to the increasingly forlorn hope that their loved ones could still be alive, until official confirmation of their deaths arrived. Some families never got over their bereavement and the sense of loss in the community must have been quite dreadful.

A Soldier-Squire

The action on 15 June 1915 also marked the end of the male line for one local aristocratic family. Second Lieutenant George Braddyll Bigland, 1st/4th Battalion King's Own, was killed in action near Rue d'Ouvert at

Bigland Hall, pictured in 2008. (From geograph.org.uk)

the age of 23. It was reported that he fell whilst leading his men in an attack. He was the only son and heir of Editha Blanch Hinde Bigland, of Bigland Brow, Backbarrow and the late Squire, George Bigland. George had been known as the 'Soldier-Squire'.

Though the Bigland Hall estate, situated between the foot of Windermere and the head of the valley of Cartmel, was not a large one, the family of Bigland was one of the most ancient in the North. George was the last in a line of ancestors who for the past 1,000 years had served as soldiers.

Another notable member of the family, Edward Bigland (1620-1704), was a sergeant-at-law and Member of Parliament for Nottingham during Oliver Cromwell's time. Today, Cartmel Priory Church and Kendal Church still contain memorials belonging to members of the Bigland family.

George B. Bigland and his wife Audrey (née Hampson), the youngest daughter of Sir Robert Hampson of Brown Howe, Blawith.

Barrow Guardian, Saturday, 26 June 1915:

For some days past rumour has been busy concerning several officers and men of the 4th King's Own Royal Lancaster Regiment. Amongst others, Capt. W. G. Pearson, son of Mr. H. G. Pearson, solicitor and Official Receiver at Barrow, was reported killed, but official news has been received to the effect that he is 'wounded and missing'.

Similarly also Lieut. Walker, son of Mr. Walker, manager of the Manchester and Liverpool Bank,

Ramsden-square, Barrow, is officially reported 'wounded and missing.' There is still hope then that these gallant young lives may be spared, and much sympathy will go out to their parents and relatives during this anxious and trying time.

On Friday, the official list confirmed that Lieutenant Walker was wounded, and also that Lieutenant G. B. Bigland was wounded and missing.

***Barrow Guardian*, Saturday, 10 July 1915:**

The uncertainty which prevailed in the district regarding the fate of Sec. Lieut. Bigland has been cleared up, his name appearing in the casualty list issued from General Headquarters, published on Wednesday, under the heading 'Previously reported wounded and missing, now reported killed'.

Casualties at Guillemont

The south Lakeland area did not experience the same massive losses sustained by other towns such as Accrington on the first day of the Battle of the Somme. There seem to have been no local Pals Battalions, due to the low population density, and the Service Battalions of the King's Own were

Memorial to George Braddyll Bigland in Cartmel Priory.

either based in other theatres or did not see action on 1 July 1916. However, casualties in the 1st/4th Battalion were horrendous enough and the Battalion went on to sustain further casualties at Guillemont on 8 August 1916, when more than 100 men were killed. Some never got over their wounds from that day and died years later from the after-effects.

One thing that becomes apparent after June 1915 is a gradual shift in the tone and nature of the local newspaper reports. The enthusiastic letters, apparently posted home by the ordinary soldiers, seem to disappear. This was, in part, due to the tightening of the censorship laws, but it is also likely that the newspapers' readers were rapidly despairing of the ever-increasing casualty lists when weighed against the paltry military gains. The war was not turning out to be as glorious as some had hoped it would be.

War Bread

A new threat to Britain had arisen by early 1917: starvation. Millom poet Norman Nicholson was born on 8 January 1914 and he turned out to be a sickly child. Norman's father was convinced that most of the illnesses he experienced in his youth were due, primarily, to the 'war bread'. Homemakers were encouraged to use less wheat and cut down on sugar in their bread Corn syrup was used in place of sugar and shortening (a type of solid fat) was used in place of fat.

Another local woman, Marian Atkinson, aged 97 in 2003, spoke to oral historians Richard van Emden and Steve Humphries about her wartime childhood. She grew up in the Lake District and was a 12-year-old schoolgirl in 1917:

> We'd see turnips, potatoes and cabbage and we'd decide what we'd pinch on the way home. On the way back, the bigger boys used to say 'Keep your eyes rolling for the farmer'. My parents wouldn't accept anything stolen – they used to make us take it back – so we used to sit under a hedge and gnaw the vegetables like a rabbit. If we could hear the farmers' horses clip-clopping, we used to bung what we'd been eating under the hedge and go like lightning back home, large as life.

The Dock Museum in Barrow has a First World War rationing order book/pass for a soldier or sailor, issued to William Lee. It is accompanied by the following description:

It states that William Lee has permission to be absent from his quarters between the dates of 16th October 1918 and 22nd October 1918. The book contains ration stamps for a week. Three have been used. Rationing was introduced in 1918 due to the U-boat campaign that targeted supplies destined for Britain, and led to many merchant vessels being sunk.

Working-class families across Britain were helped significantly by the introduction of general food rationing in February 1918. By April, all districts, whether rich or poor, received equal shares of meat and various other foodstuffs.

CHAPTER 12

Victoria Cross Medal Holders

The Victoria Cross (VC) Medal is the highest and most prestigious award for gallantry in the face of the enemy that can be awarded to British and Commonwealth soldiers. In the First World War, 634 Victoria Crosses were awarded.

Four Victoria Cross holders of the King's Own Royal Lancaster Regiment, photographed at Bowerham Barracks, Lancaster in 1932, at a regimental reunion. (From left to right: Albert Halton, James Hewitson, Tom Fletcher Mayson and, seated, Harry Christian.)

This portrait of Victoria Cross recipient Abraham Acton was painted after his death, by John Dalzell Kenworthy (1859–1954) in 1916. (By kind permission of the Beacon Museum, Whitehaven.)

Abraham Acton's Victoria Cross. (By kind permission of The Beacon Museum, Whitehaven.)

Recipients of the Victoria Cross Medal from south Lakeland and West Cumbria

Abraham Acton was born in 1893 to Robert and Eleanor Acton of Whitehaven. Today, his Victoria Cross is displayed at the town's Beacon Museum. When he won the medal, he was just 22 years old and a Private in the 2nd Battalion, The Border Regiment. Abraham and James Alexander Smith were both awarded the Victoria Cross for their actions on 21 December 1914 at Rouges Bancs, France.

Abraham gained his medal for conspicuous bravery in voluntarily leaving his trench to rescue a wounded man, who had been lying exposed against the enemy's trenches for 75 hours. That same day he left his trench once again, spending an hour under heavy fire attempting to bring in another wounded man. He was killed in action at Festubert, France on 16 May 1915 and posthumously honoured with the VC.

Bertram Best-Dunkley, was a lieutenant colonel in the 2nd/5th Battalion, Lancashire Fusiliers. He died on 5 August 1917, aged 27, of wounds at a

High honour: Bertram Best-Dunkley.

Bertram Best-Dunkley is buried at Mendinghem Military Cemetery. (By kind permission.)

VICTORIA CROSS PRESENTED.

THE LATE LIEUT.-COL. BEST-DUNKLEY.

At Risedale House, Barrow, yesterday week, Colonel Pedley, C.B., Commander of the Barrow Garrison, presented the Victoria Cross won by the late Lieut.-Col. Bertram Best-Dunkley, pinning that coveted honour on the breast of the three months old son of the gallant officer.   Mrs. Best-Dunkley is the daughter of Mr. and Mrs. W. F. Pettigrew, Risedale, and was unable to travel up to London to receive the posthumous honour at the hands of the King.   His Majesty sent a letter to Mrs. Best-Dunkley, in which he said : "It is a matter of sincere regret to me that the death of Captain (temporary Lieut.-Colonel) Bertram Best-Dunkley, 2 5th Batt. Lancashire Fusiliers (T.F.), deprives me of the pride of personally conferring upon him the Victoria Cross, the greatest of all rewards for valour and devotion to duty.—George R.I." The presentation of the V.C. was performed in the presence of the widow, Mr. and Mrs. Pettigrew, and Miss Pettigrew, the Colonel expressing in a few words the great honour that had fallen to him.

Lieut.-Col. Best-Dunkley died on August 5th last from wounds received in action on July 31st.   He joined his regiment in 1907 as second-lieutenant, and when war broke out was at Tientsin, China.   He immediately returned to England, and, joining his battalion, went to the front in May, 1915, holding a position on the staff.   He was gazetted captain in the Regular Forces in October, 1916, and acting lieutenant-colonel while commanding a battalion on October 20th, 1916. An officer, who was with Colonel Best-Dunkley at the time he was wounded, writes :—"His conduct throughout had been magnificent, and his leadership at a difficult stage was brilliant."   Other letters mention that "he was a soldier of the noblest type, courageous and resourceful in action."   All ranks who saw him on July 31st speak with enthusiasm of his disregard of personal danger, his coolness and discretion.

Colonel B. Best-Dunkley, who was stationed at Barrow for some time, married Marjorie Kate, second daughter of Mr. and Mrs. W. F. Pettigrew, Barrow, in October of last year.

Barrow Guardian, November 3 1917, report of Bertram Best-Dunkley being awarded the VC.

casualty clearing station in Flanders, Belgium, and he is buried at Mendinghem Military Cemetery, Belgium. At the time of Colonel Best-Dunkley's death, the 2nd/5th Battalion Territorial Force, Lancashire Fusiliers, formed part of the 164th (North Lancashire) Brigade in the 55th (West Lancashire) Division. Bertram was stationed in Barrow for some time before he went to France in May 1915.

An extract from the *London Gazette* No 30272, dated 4 September 1917, records the following description of the act that won him the Victoria Cross:

> For most conspicuous bravery and devotion to duty when in command of his battalion, the leading waves of which, during an attack, became disorganised by reason of rifle and machine gun fire at close range from positions which were believed to be in our hands. Lt Col Best-Dunkley dashed forward, rallied his leading waves, and personally led them to the assault of these positions, which, despite heavy losses, were carried. He continued to lead his battalion until all their objectives had been gained. Had it not been for this officer's gallant and determined action it is doubtful if the left of the brigade would have reached its objectives. Later in the day, when our position was threatened, he collected his battalion headquarters, led them to the attack, and beat off the advancing enemy.

Private Harry Christian was born in Pennington, Ulverston in 1892. He died in 1974 and is buried at Egremont Cemetery, West Cumbria. Harry Christian was 23 years old and a private in the 2nd Battalion, King's Own when he was awarded the VC for the following deed at Cuinchy, France. The citation on the event, published in the *London Gazette* on 3 March 1916, reads:

> For most conspicuous bravery. He was holding a crater with five or six men in front of our trenches. The enemy commenced a very heavy bombardment of the position with heavy 'minenwerfer' bombs, forcing a temporary withdrawal. When he found that three men were missing, Private Christian at once

Most conspicuous bravery: Harry Christian.

An injured Harry Christian receives his Victoria Cross from King George V.

returned alone to the crater, and, although bombs were continually bursting on the edge of the crater, he found, dug out, and carried all three men, thereby saving their lives. Later he placed himself where he could see the bombs coming, and directed his comrades when and where to seek cover.

Harry's VC is now displayed at the King's Own Royal Regiment Museum, in Lancaster.

Coniston's best known First World War hero was **Lance-Corporal James Hewitson** (born 1892), who served in the King's Own. James Hewitson's parents farmed at Waterhead Farm, Torver. He worked for his father on the family farm, as a farm labourer near Kendal and then afterwards near Preston. Three months after the outbreak of war, he enlisted.

James Hewitson was awarded the Victoria Cross in 1918. On 26 April 1918, at Givenchy, France, in a daylight attack

Gallantry: James Hewitson.

James Hewitson receives his Victoria Cross from King George V.

on a series of crater posts James had led his party to their objective, clearing the enemy from both trench and dug-outs, killing six men who would not surrender. After capturing the final objective, he saw a hostile machine-gun team coming into action against his men. Working his way round the edge of the crater, he attacked the team, killing four and capturing one. Shortly afterwards, he routed a bombing party attacking from a Lewis gun, killing six of them.

James survived the war and returned home. He is thought to have worked as a road repairer after the war. At some point, he underwent an operation to remove shrapnel from his spine and in 1954 he required a further operation to remove shrapnel from his shoulder. He attended the VC Centenery in 1956. He died on 2 March 1963 in Ulverston and is buried at St Andrew's Churchyard, Coniston. His medal is privately held.

Major Thomas Forshaw (1890–1943) was born in Barrow. Aged 25, while serving as a lieutenant in the 1/9th Battalion, the Manchester Regiment, he was awarded the VC for his actions between 7 and 9 August

1915 in Gallipoli, Turkey. The *London Gazette* of 9 September 1915 reported:

> When holding the north-west corner of 'The Vineyard' against heavy attacks by the Turks, Lieutenant Forshaw not only directed his men but personally threw bombs continuously for over 40 hours. When his detachment was relieved, he volunteered to continue directing the defence. Later, when the Turks captured a portion of the trench, he shot three of them and recaptured it. It was due to his fine example and magnificent courage that this very important position was held.

Magnificent courage:
Major Thomas Forshaw.

Thomas Forshaw later achieved the rank of major. He died on 26 May 1943 and was buried at Touchen End, Berkshire, initially in an unmarked grave, although a new stone was erected in 1994. His VC is displayed at the Museum of the Manchester Regiment. Lieutenant Forshaw was given a sword and the freedom of Barrow by the local council in 1916.

Albert Halton (1893-1971) was born in Carnforth. As a 24-year-old private in the 1st Battalion King's Own Regiment, he was awarded the Victoria Cross due to a brave action during the Battle of Passchendaele (or Third Battle of Ypres or 'Passchendaele'). On 12 October 1917, near Poelcapelle, Belgium, after the objective had been reached, he rushed forward about 300 yards, while under very heavy fire, and captured a German machine-gun and its crew which was causing heavy losses to nearby Allied troops.

He then went out again and brought in 12 German prisoners, showing the greatest disregard for his own safety. After the war, Private Halton was an ironworker until his retirement in 1961. His Victoria Cross is displayed at the King's Own Museum.

Albert Halton.

William Leefe Robinson (1895–1918) had attended school at St Bees, West Cumbria. He was born in Tolideta, South Coorg and was the son of Horace Robinson, who owned a coffee estate of Kalma Betta in Polibetta, and grandson of William Braham Robinson, Chief Naval Constructor at Portsmouth Dockyard. He became the first British pilot to shoot down a German airship over Britain during the war. For this he was awarded the Victoria Cross, and he was the first person to be awarded the medal for action which took place in the UK. On the night of 2 September 1916, over Hertfordshire, Lieutenant Robinson sighted a German airship, which was one of 16 attempting a mass raid over England.

Robinson made an attack, approaching from below and raking the airship with machine-gun fire. As he was preparing for another attack, the airship burst into flames and crashed into a field. This action was witnessed by thousands of Londoners who, as they saw the airship descend in flames, cheered and sang the national anthem. He died on 31 December 1918 at the home of his sister, the Baroness Heyking, from the effects of the Spanish Flu pandemic, to which his time as a prisoner of war in Zorndorf, Poland, and Holzminden, Germany had left him particularly susceptible. He was buried at All Saints Churchyard Extension in Harrow Weald and a memorial to him was later erected near the spot where the German airship crashed.

Tom Fletcher Mayson (1893–1958) was born in the village of Silecroft, near Millom. He was 23 years old, and a Lance-Sergeant in the 1/4th Battalion, King's Own during the First World War when the deed for which he was awarded the Victoria Cross took place. On 31 July 1917, at Wieltje, near Ypres, Belgium, when his platoon was held up by machine-gun fire, Lance-Sergeant Mayson, without waiting for orders, made for the gun, which he put out of action with bombs, wounding four of the German gunners. The remaining three gunners fled, pursued by Lance-Sergeant Mayson to a dug-out, where he killed them. Later, when clearing up a strongpoint, this non-commissioned officer

'A quiet little chap': Tom Fletcher Mayson.

Tom Fletcher Mayson's medals. (By kind permission)

once again tackled a machine-gun single-handed, killing six of the German team.

Finally, during an enemy counter-attack, he took charge of an isolated post and successfully held it until ordered to withdraw, by which time his ammunition was exhausted. His VC was left to St Mary's Church in Whicham, Silecroft, and is currently on loan to the King's Own Royal Regiment Museum. What the citation accompanying the VC does not say, is that all this killing was done by a man, who was only about 5 foot 5 inches tall, and who, by his own admission, 'was terrified and didn't know what had got into him'.

According to those who knew Tom Fletcher Mayson in later life, he never bragged about his deed, and seemed a 'quiet little chap'. In December 1917, celebrations were held in Millom and Silecroft for Tom Fletcher Mayson's homecoming. The Second World War found him serving in the local Home Guard and working at Millom Ironworks, as part of the railway gang in the shunting yard.

Victoria Cross winner **Samuel Wassall** lived in Lyon Street, Barrow. He survived the war and attended the unveiling of the cenotaph in Barrow Park on 11 November 1921, by General Sir W. Robertson. On this and subsequent Armistice Days, Private Wassall was asked to place the ex-servicemen's laurel wreath on the memorial. He was one of several other

Private Samuel Wassall won the Victoria Cross for saving the life of a fellow soldier.

Barrow veterans who were introduced to the King at Furness Abbey Station, when his Majesty and the Queen visited Barrow on 17 May 1917. Samuel Wassall was awarded the VC when serving as a Private in the 80th Regiment, for saving the life of a fellow soldier after the Battle of Isandlwana, South Africa, on 22 January 1879.

CHAPTER 13

Stories of Local War Dead

Captain **Alfred James Barrow** of the 10th Battalion, Lancashire Fusiliers, died of wounds on 24 June 1918, while a prisoner of war (POW). Barrow High School, Sedbergh/Heversham, Cambridge-educated Captain Barrow was the only son of the Mayor of Barrow, Alfred Barrow of Ulverscroft. He is buried in Niederzwehren Cemetery, Kassel (formerly Cassel), Germany, which was established in 1915 for the burial of POWs.

Alfred Barrow died in 1915, while he was a prisoner of war in Germany.

Barrow News, **4 May 1918:**

The Mayor and Mayoress have received a postcard from their son Capt. Barrow, who states that he is in hospital at Cassell [sic], suffering from a broken left thigh. He adds that he is going on favourably and is being well treated. It may be added that when Capt. Barrow was first wounded it was in the left leg.

Captain Barrow had been awarded the Military Cross in August 1917 for gallantry in the field. Prior to joining the army as a private, he had practised as a solicitor in Richmond, Surrey. At the time of Captain Barrow's capture, the 10th (Service) Battalion, Lancashire Fusiliers, formed part of the 52nd Brigade in the 17th (Northern) Division. The

Lancashire Fusiliers raised 30 battalions and was awarded 63 Battle Honours and six Victoria Crosses, losing 13,640 men during the course of the war.

Second Lieutenant Bartholemew (Bartle) Bradshaw, 3rd Battalion attached 1st Battalion, Border Regiment, was killed in action at Gully Ravine, Gallipoli on 11 June 1915, aged 33, and he is buried at Twelve Tree Copse Cemetery, Turkey. The only son of Mayor and solicitor Mr Bradshaw and Mrs Bradshaw of Fairfield, Barrow, he was educated at Sedbergh, and at University College, Oxford. Before the war he had a very promising career as a barrister.

On the outbreak of war, Bartle Bradshaw joined the Public Schools Battalion of the Middlesex Regiment with his cousin James Walter Murray, and in April 1914 he was appointed Second-Lieutenant of the 3rd Border Regiment. He went to the Dardanelles, where he arrived on 25 May 1915, and was attached to the 1st Border Regiment when he was killed.

Bartle Bradshaw died at Gallipoli, in 1915.

Bartle was an enthusiastic diarist. The diary he kept during the week between his departure from Alexandria (en route from England) and his first five days on the Gallipoli Peninsula was sent home to his parents under cover of a letter. After his death, this diary was passed on to his old school and published in *The Sedberghian* of July 1915. It is quite a detailed record and if the censor had intercepted the letter Bradshaw would have been in trouble. As it was, Sedbergh School was the beneficiary.

In the diary, Bartle writes as an interested and observant traveller, apparently determined to make the most of this unusual experience. Passing through Greek islands, Bartle is reminded of Greek mythology. Arriving at 'Stick-in-the-Mud Island' (Mudros), he is pleased with the resemblance to the Yorkshire Dales. He notes the excitement of the crew who have never been there before – 'stewards nipping away from the dining table with your fish or entrée in their hands to look out of portholes'.

The holiday mood continues in the diary after he reached his Battalion, which fortunately was then having a quiet time, since 87 Brigade had been in divisional reserve since 8 May and would remain so until 4 June. When a sergeant in his draft is slightly wounded soon after, Bartle considers it 'rather hard lines seeing he has only just arrived', reflecting his own enthusiasm for what lies ahead. There are cheerful references to meals in the officers' mess: 'just a pit covered with branches to keep the sun off and earth table down the centre'. He also describes being able to hear concerts being performed a long way off, and that it was possible to distinguish who had put on the concert, as the French sing God Save The King and then 'The Marseillaise', the English vice versa.

The countryside around Cape Helles (the rocky headland at the south-westernmost tip of the Gallipoli peninsula) appealed to Bartle. He explains that it is:

> very prolific, groves, myrtle, olives, figs or vines, a number of honest oak trees, fruit trees of every kind, raspberries, blackberries not yet ripe. The most extraordinary thing of all is the enormous variety of small wild flowers of the kind that grow on sandy rocky soil. The general effect is that of a rock garden of a square mile, a gorgeous blaze of colour. The gentle breeze through vines and myrtle groves and wild thyme and lavender is lovely. Red poppies everywhere, redder than the blood. How anyone can fight in a Garden of Eden like this beats me.

This is an interesting comment, since other accounts he gave later in the season demonstrate that, as the war tightened its grip, the glories of Helles faded. The landscape was progressively degraded in his view.

Towards the end of the week (Friday 29 May), work intrudes on Bartle's reflections. He takes his platoon in 'D' Coy out on a working party towards the hill of Achi Baba, 'sneaking up and dodging in and out since the enemy can see everything'. He has to break off from his work when a foul smell leads to the discovery of about 100 dead Turks and a German officer in a stream, 'so I left off work and started to bury them, a most unpleasant job. I marked the graves with a cross'.

About this time, a more personal note creeps in to the diary:

> I have not received any letters yet. Get a lump in my throat every time I censor a letter from my platoon, some of them are beautiful, all are honest. There were five letters to be censored today, four of them asked their people to pray for them. So do I. We've got some job to go through yet. I am enjoying it very much so far, thank you. I am fat and well and happy. The more letters I get the better . . . you don't catch me hogging around in the sun when there are any shells around, I nip into my dugout like a rabbit. You don't catch me running any unnecessary risks.

Twelve Tree Copse Cemetery, Turkey. (By kind permission)

The diary ends on 31 May and it may be that Second Lieutenant Bradshaw had no more time for writing, since on 4 June the Battalion came out of divisional reserve and into the line. This was the big 'push' which, though it did not directly involve the 1st Borders, kept them on the *qui vive*. On 10 June, the Battalion was ordered to make an attack on Turkey Trench. The attack was successful, but the next day saw the Turks retake the trench and they had to be ejected. This counter-attack was also successful, yet at some cost. Of the two officers killed, one was the Adjutant, Captain Moore, and the other was Bartle Bradshaw.

Barrow born **Private Robert Braithwaite** of the 1st Battalion King's Own, was killed in action on 7 May 1915, aged 23, near Mouse Trap Farm during the Second Battle of Ypres. Prior to the war, Robert had been working at the local shipyard as a holder-up. According to the war diary entry for 7 May, Private Braithwaite was killed in the trenches by shellfire.

He is commemorated on the Menin Gate Memorial, and it it likely that he was buried behind the trenches by his comrades. The German offensive captured this area son after Robert's death and his battlefield grave would have been lost in the subsequent fighting.

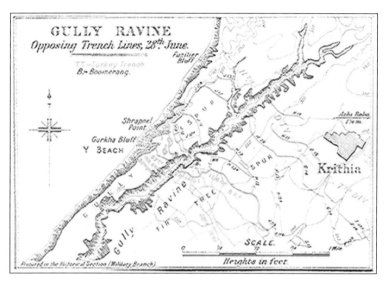

Gully Ravine, nicknamed by British troops 'The Valley of Death', presumably on account of the number of small wartime cemeteries laid out in it. (By kind permission.)

The entrance to Gully Ravine at the beginning of June 1915. It was covered with fine dry sand and plagued by flies .

'Gully Dwellers', 1915.

The remains of 'Border Block' in Gully Ravine: This feature marked the point at which the opposing Turkish and Allied trenches met. (By kind permission.)

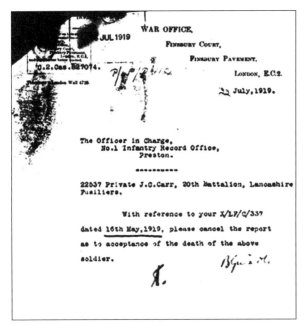

Extract from Private Joseph Charles Carr's   *Private Joseph Charles Carr.*
service records, page 19. (By kind permission.)

Private Joseph Charles Carr, 20th Battalion, Lancashire Fusiliers, was posted missing on 19 August 1916 and officially declared dead in July 1917. He had in fact deserted and was finally apprehended at Le Havre on 5 November 1918, having evaded capture for over two years. As a deserter who had evaded capture for so long, Joseph Carr could have been subject to court martial, where he would have faced the ultimate penalty of execution by firing squad – as more than 300 men did during the First World War.

However, probably because he was not apprehended until 5 November 1918, when the war was nearly over, the British Army took the decision to dispense with court martial and the only sanction Joseph appears to have faced was the forfeiture of his army pay for the period he had been absent without leave.

Before joining the army, Joseph Carr worked in the submarine dock department at Vickers. He had enlisted in August 1915, when he was only 16 years of age – and he may have still only been 16 when he was posted abroad to the British Expeditionary Force in France on 29 January 1916.

Contrary to popular belief, he would not have been under-age, as the Army routinely enlisted young men of this age, although they were not allowed to serve abroad until they reached the age of 19. Joseph Carr had lied about his age when he enlisted, claiming to be 19, thus making his enlistment illegal.

It is also notable that he enlisted at Salford, rather than in his home town of Barrow. This may have been because he was working or living in Salford, it is also possible that he had deliberately travelled there to enlist at a place where he was unknown and where his subterfuge would not be detected.

Private Edward John Cowley of the 4th Battalion King's Own died at home in Dalton on 29 April 1921, aged just 24, after a long illness. He is buried in Dalton Cemetery. It is not clear from surviving records what the nature of his final illness was and, given that he had been discharged from the army for more than two years, it is also unclear why he was eligible for commemoration by the Commonwealth Graves Commission. There is no Medal Index Card for Private Cowley, and as he did not serve overseas he was not entitled to receive any medals. However, his next of kin would still have received the commemorative Bronze Plaque and Scroll.

Private Edward John Cowley's grave.

Barrow Guardian, 16 September 1916:

On Thursday, Mr. and Mrs. Cowley, 39, Market-street, Dalton, received a note from the Infantry Record Office to the effect that their son, 15918, Pte. James Cowley, 1st Batt. Middlesex Regt., had been missing since an engagement on August 18th. Yesterday, however, two letters were received from the soldier himself, posted in France on September 10th.

As a lad of 17, in May 1914 James Cowley had joined the Territorials and so he was called up in August, on the outbreak of the war. On 15 August, his battalion moved to Slough, Berkshire to undertake guard duty on the Great Western Railway. In September 1914, like many skilled industrial workers, James Cowley was sent back to Vickers to work on munitions. The following description of the journey of the Barrow Territorials to

Slough is an extract from *The Fourth Battalion The King's Own and The Great War*, by Lieutenant Colonel F. H. A. Wadham and Captain J. Crossley:

The Battalion left Ulverston on the 15th [August], in two trains (the first at 10-30 a.m. and the second at 12 noon), and arrived at Slough at 7.30 and 10.30 p.m. respectively. The second train was delayed owing to one of the horse boxes falling to pieces at Crewe, thereby causing serious injuries to the animals it contained, and our first casualty, one of the horses being so severely damaged that it had to be shot.

On arrival at Slough the Battalion was billeted in various schools for the night, and the following morning divided up by Companies. These were distributed amongst the different stations on the length of line – from Paddington to Twyford – allotted to the Battalion. Headquarters were established at Slough, in a large empty house with spacious grounds surrounding it, which quickly acquired the sobriquet of 'Black Lead Castle', owing to one if its former occupants having rejoiced in the name of Nixey. A black cat, 'which went with the place', succeeded to the title of the former occupant.

At the stations along the line the officers and men were accommodated in the waiting rooms, without bedding, furniture, or comforts of any description, and lived in these comfortless places for rather more than three months, during which period the Battalion was carrying out the duties of patrolling the line and guarding the bridges, etc., their food being sent through from Slough in dixies. Great ingenuity was displayed by the members of the various detachments on the line in their endeavours to make their quarters, if not comfortable, at least habitable. The palm must be awarded to the Millom Detachment at Langley Park, where, under the able direction of the Company Cook, and with the assistance of a refuse tip alongside the railway, on which every conceivable kind of kitchen utensil seemed to have found its last resting place, a quite substantial and up-to-date kitchen was erected, and with the aid of a huge Beecham's Pills (or other) advertisement board and some borrowed waggon sheets, a commodious lean to shelter was constructed. The homeliness of the shelter was completed by the addition of a tame fox, with which, contrary to the usual laws of animal affection, an Airedale terrier used frequently to indulge in gambols like those of a pair of kittens.

John Henry Creber, 2nd Battalion, Durham Light Infantry, was born in Barrow in 1888. He saw service throughout the First World War and later in Russia, Turkey, India and China. His medals, which are now in the medal gallery of the Durham Light Infantry Museum, include the 1914 Mons Star, with a bar on the ribbon to show that he was one of the first men of the British Army to arrive in France, who became known as the 'Old Contemptibles'.

Buried at Finsthwaite: Franklin Benn Dearsley.

Private Franklin Benn Dearsley, 4th (Extra Reserve) Battalion, Lancashire Fusiliers, died at home at Stott Park on 10 August 1916, aged 27, from Bright's Disease. He is buried at Finsthwaite (St Peter's) Churchyard. The 4th (Extra Reserve) Battalion, Lancashire Fusiliers, remained in the UK for the duration of the war, and at the time of Private Dearsley's enlistment, they formed part of the Barrow Garrison.

There is no Medal Index Card for Frank Dearsley. He did not serve overseas and therefore was not entitled to receive any medals. He also died before the Silver War Badge was instituted and these were not issued posthumously, but his next of kin would have received the commemorative Bronze Plaque and Scroll. Tragically, a week before Frank Dearsley died he had got married.

Deaths at Home

Most of the war dead buried in Barrow died in local hospitals, which were situated on North Lonsdale, Devonshire Road and Cambridge Street. Schoolchildren were sent to other premises while local school buildings were used as hospitals. The deaths of most servicemen in British hospitals were caused by illness rather than battle injuries. One exception is a local man, **Corporal Gilbert Fell**, aged 25, of the King's Own, who was knocked down by the 10.20pm train from Southport to Liverpool. He was returning to camp after a visit to the Wesleyan Club for soldiers at Formby.

Private Nicholas Fell, 1st/4th Battalion King's Own, died at his Barrow home in March 1921, aged 27. The cause of his discharge from the army was recorded as due to 'wounds' and, given his date of discharge, it is probable that he was wounded at Guillemont on 8 August 1916.

Captain James Fisher, 4th Battalion King's Own, died of pneumonia at Liverpool on 23 February 1919, aged 24, possibly a victim of the Spanish Flu epidemic. He was eligible for the 1914-15 Star, the British War Medal and the Victory Medal. An application for the award of his 1914-15 Star was made on 14 January 1919, while he was still alive.

Prior to the war, Captain Fisher had been serving his apprenticeship as an engineer at Vickers. He took a great interest in the Territorials, and immediately on the outbreak of hostilities he joined the 4th Battalion King's Own, subsequently proceeding to France, where he served in 1915 and 1916. In the latter year he was invalided home, suffering from shell shock, and on being classified as unfit for foreign service he was attached to the 15th South Lancashire Regiment, which dealt with the loading and unloading of steamers at Liverpool.

Captain Fisher was only demobilised a fortnight prior to his death, and was about to take up work in Liverpool. His father James Fisher of Abbey Road, Barrow was Mayor of Barrow for two terms from 1894 to 1897, and 1902 to 1903.

Lance-Corporal Thomas Gregory, Royal Lancaster Regiment, signed up shortly after leaving St James Boys' School, Barrow and was killed in action in 1917. A collection of objects relating to his war service has been donated to the Dock Museum, including his Victory Medal, British War Medal, studio portrait photographs of him in uniform, a covering letter from Buckingham Palace, along with his memorial scroll and letter. All of these artefacts except the medals can be seen online through the Dock Museum collections database (*dockmuseum.org.uk*).

Second Lieutenant Hilary Loraine Heelis (born 1898) was the nephew of Beatrix Heelis, better known by her maiden name of Beatrix Potter. He was educated at Appleby and Windermere Grammar Schools and joined the army on 1 June 1916, as a private soldier, giving his prior occupation as 'school lad'. He became an officer with the Lancashire Fusiliers in 1917 and was taken prisoner in France on 4 June 1918, during a trench raid. He returned to Britain and died, aged 40, in Bolton.

Ordinary Seaman George Hoggarth was born on 10 July 1896 at Barrow, but at the time of his death he was a crew member on board the destroyer HMS *Mounsey*. The ship was sold in 1921 and was broken up, ironically, in Germany. George Hoggarth had volunteered to service in the navy and enlisted in August 1915 at Huddersfield, whilst he was working for the Mirfield Colliery Company; previously he had been employed in the shipyard at Barrow, which probably explains his decision to join the navy.

Although George came through the Battle of Jutland unscathed, he was drowned during routine operations. On Sunday 8 October 1916, HMS *Mounsey* left the naval base at Scapa, in the Orkneys, for an exercise. The following day, in conjunction with HMS *Erin*, the *Mounsey* carried out exercises, commencing at 2pm. The ship log records that, at 5.30pm, a man was reported overboard on the port side: this was George Hoggarth. The ship was stopped and the lifeboat launched. A search was carried out at slow speed for the next 40 minutes, but to no avail. No trace could be found of George Hoggarth. At 6.10pm, the ship rejoined the flotilla and returned to Scapa the next day.

George Hoggarth, who was 20 years old at the time of his death, has no known grave and is commemorated on the Plymouth Naval Memorial. The Plymouth Memorial lists the names of 7,256 men of the Royal Navy who were lost at sea and have no known grave.

George Hudson, of Ainslie Street, Barrow, was awarded the Military Cross and also held the rare distinction of having fought on the Somme in both world wars. As the *News & Star* reported (on 1 August, 2009),in 1984, aged 92, George said of his war service: 'At the end of the war I did not have a friend who went out with me. All had been killed, wounded, or transferred to other units. My main memory is of the comradeship, which I have attempted to maintain.'

Private George Matthew Knight, born at Ulverston in 1894, was working in a fish restaurant at Millbridge, Skipton at the time of his enlistment. After enlisting under the Derby Scheme (men who voluntarily registered their name under the scheme would be called upon for service only when necessary) at the end of 1915, he was called into service with his personal choice of unit, the Coldstream Guards, in July 1916 and arrived in France in January 1917. After taking part in the Third Battle of Ypres and the Battle of Cambrai in 1917, George was wounded in action during the German counter-attack at Cambrai. He died of wounds in 21 Casualty Clearing Station at Ytres, Pas-de-Calais on 2 December 1917. He is now buried in Rocquigny-Equancourt Road British Cemetery at Manancourt, France.

Lance Corporal Ernest Lewis of Finsthwaite was killed in action in France, aged 21. He joined the 9th Seaforth Highlanders in August 1914. On the outbreak of war he had been working as under-butler to **Lieutenant Colonel Timothy Fetherstonhaugh** (1869–1945) of the College, Kirkoswald (about nine miles from Penrith, Cumbria), an officer who won distinction in the field. Lieutenant Colonel Fetherstonhaugh, in a reply to a request for money from his local village church (printed in the *Otautau Standard and Wallace County Chronicle*, New Zealand in 1915), was critical of Kirkoswald's short roll of honour and, he felt, unpatriotic spirit.

The Barrow Salvation Army Citadel on Abbey Road sent 38 men to the forces and only one failed to return home. **Lance Corporal Norman MacKenzie**, a Salvation Army bandsman, 1st/4th Battalion King's Own, died on 3 August 1916, aged 21. He was the son of William and Mary MacKenzie of Union Street, Barrow. In 1921, a ceremony was held at the Citadel, Barrow to unveil a copper and bronze plaque in his memory. Norman MacKenzie was killed in action near Guillemont, during the Battle of the Somme, and his Medal Index Card notes that he died of wounds. He was eligible for the 1914-15 Star, the British War Medal and the Victory Medal.

The *Barrow Guardian* of 19 August 1916 described a local memorial service for Lance Corporal MacKenzie, held soon after his death:

> The band and corps paid their last token of love and respect to Norman MacKenzie on 12th August, by holding a memorial service. They played the Dead March in 'Saul', also 'My Guide' selection, which was one of deceased's favourites. He had done his duty and earned a true soldier's reward and left a widowed mother and one sister to mourn his loss.

Lance Corporal Jonathan Whitehead Mason, of the 21st Division Cyclist Company, Army Cyclist Corps, had been discharged from the army on 19 June 1916, as no longer physically fit for war service. He committed

SS Cambria: *the ship that brought Jonathan Mason home from France.*

suicide at home in Lonsdale Road, Millom on 13 July 1917, aged 22 and was found hanging in a stable adjoining the house. He was eligible for award of the 1914-15 Star, the British War Medal and the Victory Medal. Additionally, he had been awarded the Silver War Badge, in recognition of his honourable discharge.

Millom Gazette, 12 July 1918:

The Coroner said his [Lance Corporal Whitehead Mason's] was an especially sad case because deceased was a fine young man who had done his best to assist his country in its time of need. In August 1914, he was wounded in action by shrapnel and also had a gunshot wound in the head. He was seriously wounded in the head twice and had many other wounds. In reply to the Coroner, his father, an ironworker of Lonsdale Road, said his son did not show any horror of the war, but it had a terrible shock upon him. Jonathan's sister Josephine said he spoke of his experiences of the war and the wounds he had received, and seemed alarmed about having to join up again. He had been called up for medical examination at Lancaster by the government. He told his father he was 'going to work on a bit'.

The Coroner said the jury had very plain evidence before them. This young man never exhibited any strangeness of demeanour, but it was evident his mind had been very much distracted by the wounds he had received, and being called up to go through a similar experience again had broken down his mind, and caused him to commit this rash act, not with any wilful intention of wickedness to himself, but he was in such a state of mind at the time that he did not know what he was doing. The Coroner suggested that deceased committed the act whilst in a state of temporary insanity.

Jonathan Mason's sister, Katherine Mason.

At the inquest into Jonathan Mason's death, there was an undignified argument, when two of the jurors were absent and the coroner said he would have to resort to fining them. A juryman responded that 9.30am was a somewhat unusual time to hold an inquest. The coroner retorted that he did not think the people of Millom were such sleepy folk that they could not get up by 9.30am.

Mr and Mrs Mason lost three sons within 18 months. James's brother George, aged 19, a machineman employed at Vickers, died in an accident in the new shell shop, when his head was nearly severed. **Corporal Thomas Mason**, aged 27, of the King's Own, died in hospital as the result of injuries received upon the railway line at Plymouth. He seemed to have attempted to take a short cut across the line. He had been in the Millom Territorials when war broke out and was discharged as medically unfit, but had later re-joined before his death.

Alexander Murray McLean, son of Donald and Charlotte McLean of Steamer Street, Barrow, is commemorated on the Barrow Civic War

Memorial. A deck hand on HMS *Ascot*, the last warship lost in the war, he was killed in action on 10 November 1918, aged 21. He is also commemorated on the Plymouth Naval Memorial.

Company Quartermaster-Sergeant Hubert William Page, 1st/4th Battalion King's Own, was killed by shellfire, aged 37, near Windy Corner, Festubert on 29 May 1915 and is buried at Le Touret Military Cemetery, France. He was the husband of Agnes Page of Park Avenue, Barrow and the couple had a baby daughter. From Hubert's Service Number it can be deduced that he had enlisted before the war, and transferred over from the Volunteer Force when the Territorials were formed in 1908. He was, by profession, an engineering draughtsman at Vickers.

Killed near Festubert: Hubert Page's gravestone in France. (By kind permission.)

The *Millom Gazette* of 4 June 1915 also reported the following deaths of local men which occurred on 29 May: **Private Edward Fisher**, **Private George Taylor**, aged 19, **Colour Sergeant Hopkinson** and **G.F. Fryer**.

Private William Postlethwaite, 1st/4th Battalion King's Own, was killed in action near Arras on 10 May 1916, aged 25, alongside **Private Jack Logan** and several other Barrow men whose deaths were reported. His parents, George and Martha Postlethwaite, of Smeaton Street, Ulverston, kept the Welcome Inn in Ulverston for many years.

Barrow Guardian, 20 May 1916:

Private Postlethwaite was employed at Messrs. Case and Company's vaults at Ulverston, and just prior to re-enlisting was working at the Barrow Shipyard. The sad news of his death, [which] occurred on Wednesday last week, was contained in letters from the Lieutenant of his Platoon, and his uncle, Pte. William Postlethwaite, who was with him at the time.

Killed near Arras: Private Postlethwaite. (By kind permission)

Leonard Ford Raybould, a member of No. 7 Company, Lancashire and Cheshire Brigade, Royal Garrison Artillery, would have been involved in the action against *U-21* in January 1915. Barrow-born Leonard was in the army when it was mobilised in August 1914, as he was in a Territorial Regiment. When the shortage of munitions worsened, he was brought back to the workshop. It seems that Leonard repeatedly attempted to get into the Air Force, but owing to poor eyesight he was rejected.

He finally went to sea as an engineer and died, aged 25, while serving on SS *Innisfallen*, as a result of an attack by the German submarine *U-64* on 23 May 1918. *Innisfallen*, owned at the time by City of Cork Steam Packet, had been on a voyage from Liverpool to Cork with general cargo. Ten people were lost.

Ideal shipmate: Third Engineer Leonard Ford Raybould died at his post in the engine room.

Barrow News, **8 June 1918:**

> The following is an extract from a letter received by his parents, of Croslands Park, Barrow, from Mr WS Collister, chief engineer, Mr RL King, second engineer, and Mr John M Miller, the chief officer: "At the time of the attack, your son was on watch. As she was struck between the engine and the boiler rooms, not a man below was saved, the vessel going down in four minutes. The gallant action of your son in stopping the engines in face of death before looking for his own safety was the means of saving a considerable portion of the crew that were on deck. It may be consoling for you to know that he died a hero's death."

The King, acting on the recommendation of the President of the Board of Trade, made a posthumous award of the Silver Medal for gallantry in saving life at sea, in recognition of the gallantry displayed by Leonard Ford Raybould. The medal was presented to his parents in 1919.

Mr Robert King, the *Innisfallen*'s Third Engineer, gave the following account of the disaster in the *Barrow News*:

> When the explosion occurred I was asleep in one of the state rooms, and was completely knocked out of my bunk, being thrown onto

SS Innisfallen*: Built by Wigham Richardson & Co, Newcastle in 1896.*

the floor. I then saw that the floor of the room has been burst up and the room all wrecked. I crawled out on my hands and knees, and when I got on deck saw a raft. The Innisfallen was at this time nearly submerged, the afterdeck being awash. After some time I reached the raft, on which I found the chief steward, a sailor and a gunner, and just as I climbed on to it I saw the Innisfallen go under.

Another survivor, Able Seaman J. C. Twomey, stated:

Several of us managed to get hold of lifebelts, but I could not get mine on before the boilers exploded. Some of the boats were smashed and 11 of us succeeded in getting into a boat that afterwards capsized, and we were all flung into the water. I then grasped the keel of an upturned boat and got astride it, and after some time I saw other survivors in another boat and hailed then, and soon afterwards they hauled me aboard. While I was clinging to the capsized boat, the submarine came to the surface quite close. She was a very large one, camouflaged all over with different coloured stripes, and about 30 of her crew were on deck, who in the most callous manner were looking on, jeering and laughing, until smoke was seem on the horizon, when she suddenly submerged and made off.

The source of the smoke proved to be HM destroyer *Kestrel*, which arrived on the scene shortly after *Innisfallen* went down and ultimately rescued 24 survivors from the rafts and boats. The destroyer dropped several depth charges, attempting to hit the submarine and searched around the scene of the calamity, in the hope of finding other survivors, but nothing was seen except floating wreckage. She then proceeded to Dublin and landed the survivors at the North Wall. The ship's second officer and a fireman were detained in hospital in Dublin, owing to injuries received. Eleven men, including Leonard Raybould, were lost.

Albert Communal Cemetery Extension, France became the final resting place for two Barrow soldiers who both fought on the Somme. **Private Thomas Stanley Roseveare** served with the 10th Battalion of the Royal Fusiliers and his parents lived at Ramsden Street, Barrow. He was killed at the age of 18 on 10 July 1916, just over a week into the Battle of the Somme. Nearby is **Lance Corporal William Hartley,** who was killed, aged 24, on 6 November 1916. He was born in Barrow, but before the war he had emigrated to Australia and so he served with the 17th Battalion of the Australian Infantry. At Serre Road No 2 Cemetery, north-east of Albert, is **Thomas Cheery Eccles**, a postman from Bootle, West Cumbria, who had lived at Holborn Hill, Millom before the war. He died, aged 24, on 16 August 1916, while serving with the King's Own.

Private John Troughton, 10th Battalion, Royal Fusiliers, died on 19 March 1919, aged 24, at Orton Military Hospital, Epsom, Surrey after repatriation as a prisoner of war. Private Troughton, of Salthouse Road, Barrow, is buried at Barrow Cemetery.

Barrow News, **22 March 1919:**

He went out to France and was captured by the Huns in September last year at Cambrai. After the signing of the armistice he reached 'Blighty' on Christmas Eve, and was in such a state of health that

Prisoner of War: John Troughton, died in 1919. (By kind permission.)

he had to be taken to the Orton Military Hospital, Epsom. In civil life he was a bricklayer's labourer.

Private Edward Haslam Tyson, F Battalion Tank Corps, born in Cark-in-Cartmel, was killed in action on 27 November 1917 near Fontaine-Notre-Dame during the Battle of Cambrai. He is likely to have been in the *F30,* one of a group of F Battalion tanks which went missing. The tank had a shell hole just behind the starboard sponson and this might have killed one or more gunners.

Captain George Henry Vaughan-Sawyer of Millom, the only son of Colonel George Vaughan-Sawyer, was killed whilst on active service with the Indian Army on 27 October 1914, aged 38. He had been connected with the Indian Army for a number of years before retiring at the rank of Captain. On the outbreak of the war, he rejoined his regiment and acted as an interpreter. The *Millom Gazette* of 6 November 1914 reported that: 'He enjoyed the reputation of a distinguished author, one of his books *Sport of Gods* being in the local Lending Library. He was the husband of Dr Ethel Vaughan-Sawyer (London).'

Major General Sir Louis Vaughan (1875–1942), the second son of Cedric Vaughan, a justice of the peace and managing director of the Hodbarrow Mining Company, Millom was another officer of the Indian Army. He had distinguished himself in a succession of appointments before and during the First World War. He was educated at Uppingham and Sandhurst and, in 1896, he joined the Indian Army as an officer in the 2nd Battalion 7th Gurkha Rifles. When the war broke out, he was General Staff Officer, 2nd grade at the War Office in London, with the rank of major.

By 1917, aged just 41, Vaughan had risen to Chief of Staff Third Army, with the rank of Major-General. After the war, he served in the Third Anglo-Afghan War of 1919 and then held several army positions in India until his retirement. He died in 1942 at Broadmead, Folkestone at the age of 67. Sir Philip Gibbs commented, in *The Realities of War* (1920): 'I saw General Louis Vaughan ... That charming man, with his professional manner, sweetness of speech, gentleness of voice and gesture, like an Oxford Don analysing the war correspondence of Xenophon.'

Vaughan was nicknamed 'Father' by the troops who served under him, which John Bourne, of the University of Birmingham's Centre for First

World War Studies, who has researched the wartime nicknames given to British Army generals, attributes to a priestly, rather than patriarchal meaning.

Second Lieutenant Percy Cecil Vaughan, son of Cedric Vaughan, was killed in action at Ypres on 26 September 1917, aged 37. He was educated at Rugby and later at Corpus Christi College, Oxford. On leaving Oxford, he was called to the Bar. Early in 1915, he joined the Royal Naval Air Service (Anti-Aircraft Corps) and was severely injured in France on 25 September 1915.

George Henry Walker, a Lieutenant of the 1st/4th Battalion King's Own was killed in action near Rue d'Ouvert, France on 16 June 1915, aged 20. He was the son of George and S.A. Walker of Birkdale, Lancashire.

Lieutenant George Henry Walker.

***Barrow Guardian*, Saturday 26 June, 1915:**

In action near Rue d'Ouvert, the Territorials took part in an attack under conditions that were trying in the extreme, entering the German trenches and besting the Germans in hand to hand fighting. Official word was received in Barrow on Tuesday that two officers, Captain WG Pearson and Lieutenant Walker, were wounded and missing.

Private Richard Wilson, born at Ulverston in 1881, was employed as a gardener for Mr R. Garnett, in Low Bentham, Yorkshire at the time of his enlistment. Conscripted into the Army Service Corps at Lancaster in August 1916, he was stationed at Winchester for much of his service (broken only by a short spell in Ireland during the late autumn of 1917). In mid-January 1918, he began to feel unwell and was admitted into Hursley Military Hospital, Winchester, where he died from the effects of an over-strained heart on 3 February 1918. He is buried in All Saints Church Cemetery at Hursley, Hampshire.

Abraham Woodhouse, Leading Seaman, HMS *Amphion*, was killed in action on 6 August 1914, aged 25. He was the son of Arthur and Mary Woodhouse of Buxton Street, Barrow, and is commemorated on the Barrow Civil Memorial and the Plymouth Naval Memorial, Devon.

Brothers Lost in the Great War:
The loss of any child is greatly mourned by their parents, and during the
First World War some families would lose more than one son or daughter
to the horrors of war.

John Cloudsdale, 24, and **Thomas Cloudsdale**, 27, both serving with the
1/4th Battalion King's Own, died on 8 August 1916. The sons of Richard
Cloudsdale, of Oubas Hill, Ulverston, the brothers have no known graves
and both are commemorated on the Thiepval Memorial to the Missing of
the Somme. Thiepval was one of the fortress villages held by the Germans
on the Somme front in 1916.

At the time of the unveiling in 1932, 73,357 names were
commemorated here; the slight decrease to 72,116 today represents the
identification of bodies since then, resulting in soldiers no longer being
classified as 'missing'. Some additional names omitted from the original
list of commemorations have, however, also been added.

Edward Hannah, 19, and **Robert Hannah**, 22, died on 16 August 1917.
Sons of Robert and Jessie Hannah of Abbey Road, Barrow, both were
serving as Second Lieutenants. Edward, formerly a ranker with the
Honourable Artillery Company, was of the 1st but attached to the 6th
(Service) Battalion of the King's Shropshire Light Infantry. He had been
awarded the Military Cross in May 1916 for an act of gallantry when all
the other officers had become casualties in an assault and he took
command, consolidated the captured trench and established posts to
protect his flank.

Robert Hannah, a former Trooper of the Cumberland and
Westmorland Yeomanry, was with the 7th (Service) Battalion of the
Royal Irish Rifles at the time of his death. The brothers have no known
graves and are commemorated on the Tyne Cot Memorial to the Missing,
outside Passchendaele in Belgium. The name 'Tyne Cot' was apparently
coined when the Northumberland Fusiliers spotted a resemblance
between the German concrete pill boxes (dug-in guard posts with
horizontal loopholes for machine guns at surface-level) and typical
Tyneside workers' cottages.

John Hart, (born 1890), died on 26 October 1918, presumably during the
battle for Querenaing (in the Pas de Calais). He was originally with the
1st/4th Battalion King's Own, with the service number 3144, which was

changed to 200800 as part of the army-wide re-numbering of the Territorial Battalions in 1917. He is buried in Denain Communal Cemetery, Germany.

His brother **Stephen Hart** was serving with the Loyal North Lancashires. At the time of the 1911 Census, Stephen had been living at Hindpool and is listed as son of George and Emma Hart of Dalton. Stephen died of wounds before his brother, on 27 June 1916. In a memoriam notice, June 1917:

> In loving memory of Private Stephen Hart, Loyal North Lancashires. Sleep on, dear son, in a far off grave, A grave we may never see, But as long as life and memory lasts, I will remember thee, I think of him in silence, no eyes may see me weep, He sleeps beside his comrades, in a hallowed grave unknown, But his name is written in letters of gold, In the hearts he loved at home. Deeply mourned by his mother and father, and sisters and brothers, also his brother John in France.

A third Hart brother, **George Henry Hart** (born 1898), was serving with the 3rd Battalion King's Own Royal Lancaster when he died on 11 October 1918. He is listed simply as G. Hart in the Commonwealth War Graves Commision list. Records of the King's Own Royal Regiment Museum show that he died at home, probably never having served abroad. The 3rd Battalion was the pre-war Special Reserve/Depot battalion and George Henry Hart is noted as having been with them when he died.

Private Samuel Hunt, 20th Battalion, King's Liverpool Regiment – the Liverpool Pals, was originally from Barrow. He died, aged 25, on 30 July 1916 when the Regiment was virtually wiped out attacking Guillemont on the Somme battlefield. His brother **Private Septimus Hunt**, who served with the Cameronians, also lost his life in the war. He died on 13 October 1917 during the opening stages of the Battle of Paschendaele. He is buried in the Commonwealth War Graves Commission Cemetery in the Belgian village of Poelcapple. Both the Hunt brothers worked at Withnell Fold Paper Mill, Chorley and are commemorated in the Parish Church of St James, Brindle, Lancashire.

Edward Nicholson, 29, and **William Nicholson**, 18, were both serving with the 1/4th Battalion King's Own when they died on 8th August 1916.

They were the sons of Benjamin and Sarah Nicholson of Fell Croft, Dalton, and as have no known graves. The brothers are commemorated on the Thiepval Memorial to the Missing.

Captain James Thurstin Wright, Royal Navy Air Service, died on 17 July 1919. He was stationed at Barrow from March 1918 until his death, as a result of a motorcycle accident in July 1919. It is believed he was associated with the building and operation of naval airships at Vickers. As indicated on his headstone in Barrow Cemetery, his brother was also killed in the war. **Private Basset Wright**, educated at Marlborough College and at Oriel College, Oxford, is commemorated on the Thiepval Memorial.

CHAPTER 14

Finding Lost Heroes

The number of servicemen commemorated on the official register of the First World War dead (i.e. those individuals commemorated by the Commonwealth War Graves Commission) has been steadily rising over the last few years. By February 2014 it included 1,117,091 soldiers from Britain and the Commonwealth.

It has transpired that, in the old days of paper files and card indexes, quite a few men who were killed in action were overlooked for commemoration, and this oversight is now being corrected. Of course, after such a long passage of time there is little chance of identifying their graves. Instead, their names are added to the existing official memorials that populate the First World War battlefields, according to where they fell.

Other names have been added as a result of the identification of men who were discharged from the forces and subsequently died as a result of wounds or sickness contracted during their service. Usually their graves can be found in local cemeteries: if no headstone is present, then arrangements will be made for one to be erected.

Daniel Cowen, 1st (Garrison) Battalion, Essex Regiment, died at home in Ulverston on 7 March 1918, aged 40, from pulmonary tuberculosis and is buried at Dalton Cemetery. Before joining the army, he was employed as a furnace man. During Private Cowen's service in Egypt, the 1st (Garrison) Battalion, Essex Regiment, was deployed as Line of Communication troops, supporting the forces protecting the Suez Canal against attack by the Turkish Army. It is believed that he served in this unit at Gallipoli too.

Daniel Cowen was eligible for the 1914-15 Star, the British War Medal and the Victory Medal. He was awarded the Silver War Badge, in recognition

HD 116703

CERTIFIED COPY of an	ENTRY OF DEATH
Pursuant to the Births and	Deaths Registration Act 1953

	Registration District				Ulverston				
1918 .	Death in the Sub-district of	Dalton			in the	County of Lancaster			
Columns	1	2	3	4	5	6	7	8	9
No.	When and where died	Name and surname	Sex	Age	Occupation	Cause of death	Signature, description, and residence of informant	When registered	Signature of registrar
347	Seventh March 1918 53 Fell Croft, Dalton u.D.	Daniel COWEN	Male	40 Years	No occupation No. 22633 Ex- Private Essex Regt. Army Pensioner	1. Pulmonary Tuberculosis. 2. Asthenia No P.M. Certified by R.H. Fothergill M.B.	Mary Ann Cowen Widow of deceased Present at the death 53 Fell Croft, Dalton	Eighth March 1918	I.W. Johnstone Registrar

Certified to be a true copy of an entry in a register in my custody.

Superintendent Registrar

25th January 2008

Date

CAUTION: THERE ARE OFFENCES RELATING TO FALSIFYING OR ALTERING A CERTIFICATE AND USING OR POSSESSING A FALSE CERTIFICATE. © CROWN COPYRIGHT

WARNING: A CERTIFICATE IS NOT EVIDENCE OF IDENTITY.

Daniel Cowen's headstone and his death certificate. (By kind permission.)

of an honourable discharge as a consequence of his sickness. His death due to war service was not officially recognised until February 2008. The cards record his discharge on 3rd August 1917, but not the date of his death and include no correspondence address details. His name was finally added to the Commonwealth War Graves Commission's database on 17 June 2008, and a headstone was erected for him in Dalton Cemetery in 2009.

One more name beside that of Daniel Cowen was added to the war memorial in Barrow Park in 2009. Over 95 years later, the death of Barrow **Private Joseph Henry Park**, an Old Contemptible of the 1st Battalion of the Cheshire Regiment, was officially commemorated. Like many Barrow men, Joseph Henry Park had begun his working life at Vickers and was killed on active service in 1914.

Private Park's name was added after research by his relatives Clifford Moffet and his son Nigel showed without doubt that he qualified to be recorded among the town's war dead. The Commonwealth War Graves Commission provided details of the date he died and the cemetery in France where he is buried.

Unknown to the Authorities

Occasionally, evidence emerges that a First World War soldier who is listed on an official memorial as 'grave unknown' in fact has a grave in a civic cemetery previously unknown to the authorities. In these cases, the Commonwealth War Graves Commission changes the place of commemoration in its official database.

James Huddleston (served as Brooks), 4th Engineering Officer, Mercantile Marine, SS *Tuscan Prince*, died on 5 August 1918, aged 23, when his ship was torpedoed in the English Channel by *UC-49* (one of 64 submarines of the UC II class). His body was recovered and brought to Barrow Cemetery for burial. He is listed as J. Brooks on the Barrow War Memorial. Until March 2009, he was officially commemorated on the Tower Hill Memorial, London. This memorial commemorates men and women of the Merchant Navy and Fishing Fleets who died in both World Wars and who have no known grave.

It would appear that James Huddleston's mother had died when he was still a baby and so his father had arranged for him to be brought up by his maternal aunt and uncle. He subsequently assumed their surname, although whether he was ever formally adopted by them is unknown. The Commonwealth War Graves Commission inaccurately lists his parents as John and Helen Huddleston.

The SS Tuscan Prince *entered service in 1913.*

CHAPTER 15

Their Names Live Forevermore

Civic memorials to those lost in the First World War are usually fairly straightforward to locate, as they were generally erected in prominent places. Additional memorials are also located in churches, and yet more in buildings that may not be readily accessible to the public. There are also war memorials that have now fallen into disuse and have been stored away, so that as a result they are no longer visible; these require the most persistence to locate.

Not everyone who lost a close relative in the First World War wanted their relative's name to appear on a memorial. One mother described in a letter, now preserved in Lancashire Record Office, that she felt this would merely act as a reminder of her loss every time she passed it.

The realisation of the common sacrifice made by those from all backgrounds who served in the First World War and the corresponding need for equality of commemoration was one of the guiding principles of Major General Sir Fabian Ware (1869–1949), the *de facto* founder of the Imperial War Graves Commission, now the Commonwealth War Graves Commission. With very few exceptions (less than 30, the most celebrated being the Unknown Soldier buried in Westminster Abbey), repatriation of the dead from battlefields abroad was prohibited, irrespective of how illustrious the victim (this prohibition even included a grandson of Queen Victoria). They were also to be given the same memorials, with a general receiving an identical headstone to a private soldier.

Furthermore, there were to be no class divisions when it came to burial,

The unveiling of the Barrow Civic War Memorial in 1921.

with officers buried alongside their men. The only notable exception occurred at the base hospital of Etaples, where officers were buried in a separate plot during the war and the arrangement was left unchanged when the formal cemetery was constructed.

Barrow War Memorial

Barrow's War Memorial in Barrow Park was unveiled on 11 November in 1921 by Field Marshall Sir William 'Wullie' Robertson (1860–1933) and records almost 600 names of those who fought and died in the First World War. There is no official figure of Barrow residents who served in the conflict, but a realistic estimate of the number who survived the war is around 3,000, yet many of those who returned had been disabled by their injuries.

'Wullie' Robertson is the only soldier to have enlisted as a Private and retired as a Field Marshall – a testament to his widely acknowledged ability. He was never ashamed of his humble roots and is said to

Field Marshall Sir William Robertson, pictured in 1915.

have continued to 'drop his aitches' all throughout his life. After the reverses at the Second Battle of Ypres (21 April to 25 May 1915), he was detailed to sack the unfortunate Lieutenant General Sir Horace Smith-Dorrien. He apparently did so with the phrase, 'Orace, you're for 'ome!'

It seems quite fitting that it was Wullie Robertson who unveiled the memorial as, of all the General Staff, he would have understood the lives of the enlisted Barrovian men the most. In 1930, he also unveiled a memorial in Southampton to those servicemen who have no known grave and still lie 'somewhere in the unplumbed and estranging sea'.

The Barrow War Memorial commemorates three men who served with the Royal Army Medical Corps (RAMC): Private David Finlay, 18th Field Ambulance, died on 28 September 1916 and is buried at Barrow Cemetery; Private John Peter Kayes, 15th Field Ambulance, was killed in action on 26 June 1918 and is buried in Tannay British Cemetery, Thiennes, France; Private Joseph William Pattinson, 21st Field Ambulance, died of wounds on 12 May 1915 and is buried at Boulogne Eastern Cemetery, France. The Royal Army Medical Corps was responsible for medical care throughout the First World War, attempting to maintain the health and strength of the forces in the field, and treat the sick and the injured.

Barrow's War Memorial lists people from all walks of life; there is no distinction of rank, nor prominence given to civic importance. This tends to be the case for all war memorials, although there are examples where officers may be listed first. The war was a great social leveller and most memorials were financed, at least in part, by public subscription. The perpetuation of class distinction among those who were lost would have received short shrift from an embittered population.

In the Barrow Archive and Local Studies Centre there is a list of all the names inscribed on war memorials in the area of 'Lancashire North of the Sands'. This list indicates that there were once other names on the memorial which are now no longer present. The reason for this is not clear.

Submariners who lost their lives during the First World War were remembered in Barrow in 2009, as two memorial benches were unveiled in the Coronation Gardens on Abbey Road. Members of the Barrow Submariners' Association paid tribute to their late comrades during a short service.

A tribute was also created in Ramsden Square to mark the coincidental centenary and fiftieth anniversary of the Australian Submarine Service and the Barrow Branch of the Submariner's Association. Barrow has strong

This memorial marks the centenary of the launch of Australia's first two submarines at Barrow and the fiftieth anniversary of the founding of the Barrow Branch of the Submariners Association. (Taken by the author, 2013)

links with Australia, as the country's first two submarines, *AE1* and *AE2*, were built at the town's shipyard. A new memorial was unveiled by Admiral the Lord Boyce (Lord Warden of the Cinque Ports and Patron of the Submariners Association) and James, Lord Abinger on 18 May 2013.

The biggest war memorial in Barrow is located on Piel Island. There is no stone or monument to bear names of the dead, but a memorial stone (*pictured above*) at the end of the ferry jetty at Rampside records the fact that the island was gifted to the Borough by the Duke of Buccleuch, in remembrance of the town's losses during the war. Piel Castle stands on the south-eastern point of Piel Island. The castle is now in the care of English Heritage, and it can be reached by a ferry from Roa Island, a few miles south-east of Barrow.

Some 68 employees and former employees of the Furness Railway died during the First World War. Their memorial is on the forecourt of Barrow Railway Station. It bears scars from the Second World War, when the station suffered bomb damage in 1941, during the Barrow Blitz, the Luftwaffe bombings of the town, which chiefly occurred during April and May 1941. The shipyard was the bombers' main target. Many Barrovians

Piel Island, pictured in 1910.

Unveiled by Mayor Hazel Edwards in 1993 the memorial stone at Piel Island. (By kind permission.)

The Furness Railway War Memorial. (Taken by the author, 2013.)

Holes and gashes: The Furness Railway War Memorial. (Taken by the author, 2013.)

THE DAMAGE TO THIS MEMORIAL WAS CAUSED BY ENEMY ACTION IN WORLD WAR II   1939-1945

believe that the first sign of German interest in the town was in May 1936, when the Hindenburg Zeppelin slowly flew past, descending very low over Barrow.

Other memorials in the town can be found at: Barrow Police Station; Abbey Road Post Office; Furness Academy (formerly Barrow Grammar School for Boys); Alfred Barrow School; Hawcoat Memorial Hall; the Cemetery Cottages plaque; Roose School; five memorials in St James's Church; St John's Church Lectern Bible; and the Ernest Pass Memorial Cricket Ground (Barrow Cricket Club).

A Selection of Local War Memorials, Listed A-Z

Askam and Ireleth Civil Parish War Memorials

The Askam War Memorial is located in the memorial gardens. The names of the First World War dead are duplicated on a bronze plaque in Ireleth (St Peter's) Church, which was unveiled on 19 March 1921. There is evidence that at one time other memorials existed at various locations in the village, but they now seem to have vanished.

Captain Johnson McMillan (Jack) Challinor (d. 1928), the son of the village doctor Sam Challinor, is buried in St Peter's Churchyard. He won the Military Cross while serving with the King's Own Scottish Borderers at Hill 60, in 1915. He died in 1928 of heart failure, aged 41.

Also at Askam Churchyard is the gravestone of Francis and Maria Mailes. Francis Mailes died in 1930, his wife seven years earlier, and below their names is that of their son Charles Mailes, who was killed in action at Fampoux, France in 1917, at the age of 23.

Askam War Memorial lists 50 men who lost their lives in the First World War.

Broughton War Memorial bears the names of 21 soldiers who died from 1914–1919.

Broughton in Furness War Memorial

Among those named on Broughton War Memorial is Private Ernest Hadwin, a young country boy from Ulpha in the Duddon Valley. He was a Territorial in 1/4th Battalion King's Own. From his service number it can be deduced that he enlisted a month after war broke out, and he went to France on 3 May 1915. Four of his brothers also joined the forces: Abraham, Leonard, Robert and Thomas Hadwin.

Cark-in-Cartmel War Memorials

The following information has been sourced from *cumbrianwar memorials.blogshop.uk*:

On 19th July 1919, thousands of servicemen marched past Lutyen's temporary Cenotaph in Whitehall led by many of the wartime leaders. The Royal Navy was represented by Admiral David Beatty (1871–1936) who, in 1910, was promoted to Rear Admiral aged just 39 – the youngest non-royal to receive such an advancement since Lord Nelson. He led the First Battlecruiser Squadron at Jutland and, after two of his ships, HMS *Invincible* and HMS *Queen Mary*, blew up he uttered the immortal words "There seems to be something wrong with our bloody ships today". Beatty can be seen on the picture below; he's the one in the centre leading the main body of sailors some paces behind the boy carrying the flag. The boy with the flag was midshipman J.B. Somerset, reputedly related to the Cavendish family of Holker Hall, Cark.

Beside the paved path from Lych Gate to Cartmel Fell Church there is a slate slab mounted on a slate plinth, which is also dedicated to fallen soldiers. There are 11 names from the Great War, including three by the name of Willan. Cartmel Priory, the Priory Church of St Mary and St Michael, Cartmel has a war memorial. There are 16 names on it from the Great War.

Midshipman J.B. Somerset, carrying the flag past the temporary Cenotaph. Admiral David Beatty can be seen walking behind the flagbearer.

Dalton in Furness Civic War Memorial
There are war memorials at St Mary's Church, Dalton Methodist Church, Dalton Catholic Church (formerly an Anglican church until the 1960s), and Dalton Conservative Club. In Dalton Castle, now owned by the National Trust, there is a large unsigned brass plaque commemorating five men of the Dalton Co-operative Society who died in the First World War.

Station Road, Dalton.

Grange-over-Sands War Memorial
One of the seminal events of the Great War was the sinking of the Cunard
Liner *RMS Lusitania* on 17 May 1915 off the south coast of Ireland, while
she was making her way back to Liverpool from New York. Torpedoed
by *U-20*, she sank with huge loss of life. In the parish church at Grange,
there is a small plaque commemorating Evan Arthur Leigh (1850–1915)
of Yewbarrow Hall, Kendal, who was among the dead.

Great Gable War Memorial
The Great Gable (a mountain in the Western Fells) war memorial was
officially unveiled before 500 people, who assembled in soft rain and
rolling mist on the high crest of Great Gable on Whit Sunday, 8 June 1924.
At the outset of the ceremony, the Union Jack that once flew from HMS
Barham at the Battle of Jutland enshrouded the bronze tablet. To conclude
the ceremony, the Last Post was sounded by two buglers of the St Bees
School Cadets.

The memorial tablet reads:

> In glorious and happy memory of those whose names are inscribed
> below, members of this club (Fell and Rock Climbing) who died
> for their country in the European War, 1914-18, these fells were
> acquired by their fellow members and by them invested in the
> National Trust for the use and enjoyment of the people of our land
> for all time.

William Henry Bright Gross (1890–1916), of Greengate Street, Barrow,
is one of 20 men listed on the Great Gable Memorial. He was killed in
action on 3 November 1916 and is among the thousands with no known
grave who are commemorated on the Thiepval Memorial on the Somme.
He was a Second Lieutenant with the 1st Battalion, Queen's Royal West
Surrey Regiment. His father worked as a stationary engine driver for the
Furness Railway Company, in its carriage and wagon department.

Benjamin Heywood Whitley, also listed on the Great Gable Memorial,
served with the Royal Scots and was killed in action on the Somme near
Longueval in 1916. His parents lived at West Dene, Kilner Park,
Ulverston. B.H. Whitley was wrongly recorded as 'B.H. Witty' on the
original memorial and this mistake was rectified by the club as part of the
Fell and Rock Climbing Club's centenary celebrations in 2006.

Kirkby-in-Furness War Memorial was unveiled by the Mayor of Barrow, Colonel Wadham, on Easter Sunday 1920. The History of Kirkby Group welcomes any additional information about the men who are named on it.

Kirkby-in-Furness War Memorial

The war memorial in St Cuthbert's Churchyard, Kirkby carries the names of 30 men of the village who died for their country, 23 of them in the First World War. Names on the St Cuthbert's memorial include John Victor Cranke, who was killed on 20 April 1918 at Givency (Battle of the Lys), aged 30. He had enlisted as a Private in the Royal Field Artillery in Millom. At some point he was transferred to the 1st Battalion Northamptonshire Regiment.

His body was never found, and a further mystery surrounds the inscription of John Cranke's name on the Kirkby War Memorial. His name was apparently added after all the others. According to the *Furness Military Chronicle,* it was on a separate stone as late as 1937. The reason why John Cranke was not named on the memorial unveiled in 1920, and why he was then added, apparently after 1937, is not known.

Also commemorated are as follows: Private William Sykes, 1/4th Battalion King's Own, who worked for Furness Railway and is also named on the Furness Railway Memorial, Barrow. He was killed on 15 June 1915 at Festubert, France, aged 22, and may have been with Private Mark Gregg and Private Addison Bell.

Lance Corporal John Tyson Shepherd, 1st Battalion, King's Own, worked in the local quarry in 1913, as did his father and two brothers. (The 1st Battalion was one of two regular battalions before the war. When it was mobilised in August 1914, it was made up to strength with reservists). He was killed in action on 12 April 1917, the fourth day of the Battle of Arras, aged around 23.

Private Richard Knight of Soutergate seems to have been brought up by his grandmother (she is named as his next of kin) and he emigrated to Canada in 1911, aged 23. There he joined the Princess Patricia's Canadian Light Infantry (Eastern Ontario Regiment) and was killed on 8 May 1915, near Ypres, aged 27. He is also named on his grandparents' gravestone in St Cuthbert's Churchyard.

Private Richard Townson, 44th Company, Machine Gun Corps (Infantry), was born and lived in Kirkby. In 1911, aged 15, he was a clerk at Foxfield Station. He was killed in action on 22 August 1917 near Ypres, aged 21, and is also commemorated on the Furness Railway War Memorial at Barrow Station.

Burlington Slate Quarry, Kirkby

When first erected, the memorial was situated next to the company offices and railway track, which ran from the main line up to the quarry head. Eventually, the only way to see the memorial was to stumble over it by trespassing along the old railway line. Burlington Slate, the company who owned the quarry, took the decision to dismantle the memorial piece by piece and move it to its current position outside the company premises, refurbishing it in the process.

The Burlington Slate Quarry War Memorial commemorates seven employees of Burlington Slate who gave their lives during the Great War: Addison Bell, Edward Greenhow, Mark Gregg, Thomas Heaton, Issac Hudson, John Shepherd and Lewthwaite Shaw.

Private Mark Gregg, 1st/4th Battalion King's Own, was the son of Adam Gregg of Grizebeck, also a quarry worker. He was killed on 15 June 1915 on the first day of the Battle of Festubert, aged 30 or 31. Private Isaac Hudson, 8th Battalion King's Own (one of the King's Own four 'Kitchener' battalions of volunteers), was killed on 9 April 1917, on the first day of the Battle of Arras, aged 22. He is named on the family headstone in St Cuthbert's Churchyard. Thomas Ernest Heaton, a quarryman in 1913, was born at Woodland. He joined the 8th Battalion King's Own and was killed in action between 9-12 April 1917, in the first few days of the Battle of Arras, aged 32.

The current Burlington Slate premises, in Kirkby.

*The Lindal-in-Furness War Memorial is located at
St Peter's Church.*

Lindal-in-Furness War Memorial
This memorial lists 18 men who were killed in action or died of wounds.
Inside the church is a gothic lacquered brass plaque, which lists the lost
village men by the year in which they died .

Millom War Memorial
Hundreds of men from the Millom district fought in the First World War.
The Millom Civic War Memorial, built opposite the railway station, was
unveiled on 23 May 1925 and the official present at the unveiling was
Major General Sir Louis Vaughan, who was born in Millom.

One man listed on this memorial is the former Millom vicar's son, Lieutenant Frank Guy Buckingham Pascoe, who was the rear seat observer in a wood and canvas aircraft called an *RE8*. Lieutenant Pascoe and his pilot, Sergeant Hubert Whatley, were killed on 2 July 1917 when their plane came down in a ball of flames at Deulemont, France.

Private Edwin Chadwick, 2nd Battalion South Lancashire Regiment, was killed in action on 24 October 1914 and is commemorated on the Millom War Memorial and on the Le Touret Memorial. His occupation, as recorded in the 1901 census, was farm servant and he resided at Town End, Drigg & Carleton, Cumberland. He was born in 1883, in Millom.

Thomas Henry Tyson is buried in Millom (Holy Trinity) Churchyard.

Another man listed on the Millom War Memorial is Private Thomas Henry Tyson, who was born in Broughton. He was transferred to 411th Labour Corps Agricultural Company, and died from pneumonia at a military hospital in Derby on 11 November 1918, aged 32. Before he joined the army, Thomas Tyson was employed at the Co-operative farm at Langthwaite. It is likely that he was wounded near Delville Wood during the Battle of the Somme in July 1916 and it seems that he was transferred to the Labour Corps after recovering, his medical category then being too low for him to be sent back overseas on active service.

Leslie Urwin Tyson, 1st/4th Battalion King's Own, is also listed on the Millom War Memorial and was a former pupil of Millom Secondary School. He was killed in action on 20 September 1917, aged 19, during the Third Battle of Ypres.

The sad news of his death was conveyed to his relatives in the following letter from Lance Corporal W. G. Bosanko of Haverigg:

Dear Mr. and Mrs. Tyson,

It is with deepest regret that I have to inform you of the death of your son, Leslie Tyson. He was with us in the recent battle, and was killed by the explosion of a shell. It may be of some little comfort

Millom War Memorial.

The unveiling and dedication of Millom War Memorial, in 1925. General Sir Louis Vaughan can be seen, as can the sculptor who created the memorial, Alec Miller (second from right).

The unveiling and dedication of Millom War Memorial, in 1925. It is not known when (or why) the surrounding wall was demolished.

to you to know that he suffered no pain, death being instantaneous. I feel his loss, as he was a signaller with me, and an old-time chum. May God comfort you in your sad loss.

Tendering you my deepest sympathy,

I am, Yours sincerely,

W. G. BOSANKO.

He is buried in Bedford House Cemetery, Zillebeke, Belgium.

Millom Gazette, 29 May 1925:

Major-General Sir Louis Vaughan saluted the Memorial, then turning to his hearers immediately facing the front view of the structure, he said: 'We have assembled here today on this solemn occasion to unveil and dedicate this beautiful memorial to those gallant sons of Millom who gave their lives to there country during the Great War. In 1914, when hostilities broke out, the men of Millom were amongst the first to come forward and offer their services to their country, and during the succeeding four-and-a-half years every man in the nation was called upon to do some task for the great Empire to which we have the honour to belong.

To many the lot fell to proceed across the seas and take part in the awful fighting that continued there during the whole of the four and a half years. Some came back; others there are whose graves lay mostly in foreign countries, and who will never return. Amongst the prayers that our clergy have read to us today was that saying of our Lord's, 'Greater love hath no man than this, that a man lay down his life for his friends.' And who are the friends for whom these men, these relations of ours (husbands, fathers, brothers, other blood relations of most of who are assembled here today), whose names are inscribed upon this monument, laid down their lives? They died for the safety of the families and homes in Millom, the safety of their country – England – and the integrity of the British Empire. It is fitting that on this day, the 24th of May, the birthday of Queen Victoria of blessed memory, the day set apart and called Empire Day, we should dedicate this memorial to these gallant men who had died for their Empire.

These men who had died expected something more than that we should erect something to their memory; they had died trusting that we would complete the task in the doing of which they fell, and that task is not yet completed. There are some who think that when peace is signed prosperity and plenty will follow immediately. Alas! it is not so, has never been so, and can never be so; history tells us that after wars real peace and prosperity does not come for a very, very long time. Peace, and peace after victory brings dangers with which we have to contend and fight. Even now, seven years after the war, we are still being confronted with dangers. The Empire is faced with dangers, and we are faced with horrible difficulties, mostly of an economic type, and these can only be overcome by patience and endurance, and not expecting too much to come at once. By the wise direction of the country, but above all by the whole-hearted combination of loyalty and the spirit of citizenship could the duties which have been left by those who had died be performed. Whenever passing the memorial, or leaving Millom, the General asked that his listeners should let the thought and sight of the memorial strengthen their determination to do their duty as those who died would have them do it; 'our duty to God, our duty to our King, and our duty to our Empire'.

Councillor Youren, the Chairman of the Council at the time, commented that it was with mixed feelings that he accepted the memorial on behalf of the town's inhabitants. He regretted that civilisation had not so far advanced as to make war an impossibility, and that more peaceable and more conciliatory methods had not been adopted to settle the grievances and disputes of nations, without resorting to the follies and arbitrament of war. At the same time, he said, he rejoiced to know that, when the call came to the manhood and the womanhood of the country and liberty, so many Millom townspeople had answered the call of duty.

By the late 1980s, the original sandstone panels had become weathered and were difficult to read. Replacement panels were commissioned by the town council, but some spelling mistakes were introduced on to them by the monumental masons.

Muncaster War Memorial
This memorial in West Cumbria is a fine example of Edwin Lutyens' work. He was probably the most famous and respected British architect of his generation, and in 1913-14, Lutyens also worked on the design for Abbey House, Barrow, built to provide guest accommodation for Vickers.

The Preston Pals Memorial
Burlington Slate supplied the slate for the Preston Pals Memorial, which

was unveiled on 22 July 2012 at Preston Railway Station. Charles Pennington, born in Barrow in 1895, and Francis William Wright, born in Barrow in 1891 and who died aged 90, were members of the Preston Pals, a group of men from Preston, Lancashire and the surrounding districts who volunteered to fight in France and took part in the Battle of the Somme.

Francis William Wright was awarded a Distinguished Conduct Medal, according to the *London Gazette*, 'for conspicuous gallantry in action. In spite of resistance he, single-handedly, captured 20 of the enemy, including an officer, and brought them back to Battalion Headquarters'.

At least two Preston Pals were born in Barrow. Thomas Dennis Trees (1889–1946) was discharged on 20 January 1915 because of defective vision. His fellow Barrovian George Hunter (1883–1951) joined him in the Pals. In September 1915, exactly 12 months after their formation, the Preston Pals took part in the Battle of Loos, albeit a fairly minor part, and received their first casualties. One of the last surviving members of the Preston Pals who served in France was James Collier Nickeas. He died in 1986 in Barrow, aged 93.

Silecroft War Memorial

There are two memorials at Whicham in the parish church. Both are in the form of marble plaques, one commemorating the dead of the First World War and one to commemorate the dead of the Second World War. On the south side of the church is a plot belonging to the Caddy-Huddlestone family which contains a family headstone and two more CWGC graves. The earlier war grave is that of Private Tom Caddy who served with the Machine Gun Corps and died in March 1920.

Silverdale

Bradford Dyers' Association bought Bleasdale House, Silverdale in 1921 as a convalescent home and as a memorial to the 707 members of the association who died in the First World War, as well as the 37 killed when Low Moor Munitions, Bradford suffered an explosion in 1916. The house was built for the Sharp family, but during the war had been used as an auxiliary hospital.

Silecroft War Memorial, in the Parish of Whicham, with Black Combe in the background.

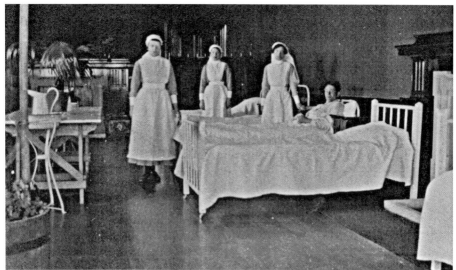

Corporal William Brabban, 18th Northumberland Fusiliers, with some nurses. He was injured on 1 July 1916 on the opening day of Battle of Somme. Shrapnel in lower spine and shell shock.

Hallthwaites War Memorial

The War Memorial at Hallthwaites (also known as 'Thwaites') contains the name of a particular local hero, Lieutenant Charles Lewthwaite, C Battery, 231 Brigade, Royal Field Artillery, who was killed in action on 29 July 1917. The 33-year-old lieutenant won the Military Cross for bravery and according to his citation: 'he showed great courage and promptness in putting out a fire which had broken out in his gun position caused by heavy hostile shell fire. He also went out into the open under heavy fire and rescued a wounded infantryman. His work at all times has been remarkably good.'

War memorial at St Anne's Church, Hallthwaites.

Ulverston War Memorial

The main war memorial in Ulverston is sited in the marketplace. It bears the names of 175 men and women of the town who died in the First World War and 59 who died in the Second World War.

The original battlefield grave marker at St Anne's Church, Hallthwaites, belonging to Lieutenant Charles Lewthwaite, who was killed in action on 29 July 1917. (By kind permission)

Ulverston Market Place in 1912. Just in front of the lamp post is the future site of the war memorial. (By kind permission)

War memorials do not accommodate the names of those who faced hardship after losing loved ones during the conflict. In Ulverston Cemetery is a simple gravestone belonging to Eleanor Dickinson, who died in 1956, aged 70. Above her name is that of her husband, Edward Dickinson, who was killed in action near Spider House Farm, Oosttaverne, during the Third Battle of Ypres, in July 1917. Eleanor was left to bring up their two children alone.

Private Harold Gardner of Ulverston appears on the market cross, and in several other places: on the name panels in the War Memorial Chapel in St Mary's Parish Church; on the memorial in Ulverston Victoria High School and on the school's photographic Roll of Honour; on his family's grave in the local cemetery; and finally on the panels of the missing at Tyne Cot Military Cemetery. He was killed, aged 19, near Armentieres on 10 April 1918, while serving with the 9th Battalion, Cheshire Regiment. He had arrived in France on 29 March. His father, Thomas, was employed as a 'Local Inspector of Nuisances'.

Unusually, there are Canadian soldiers' pictures on the Roll of Honour

(Above and below)
Unveiling and dedication of Ulverston War Memorial, 13 May 1921. The memorial was unveiled by Privates Richard Cross M.M. and A. Jones, both amputee ex-servicemen.

Tank displayed in The Gill, Ulverston, during the First World War.

at Ulverston Victoria Grammar School, including Gunner Alan Miles, who joined up in Calgary on 18 April, 1916. The 1901 census states that he was born in Egton cum Newland, Ulverston. His father earned his living as a stone carver and two of his sisters were employed as domestic servants. Alan Miles survived the war.

The Conscientious Objectors' Memorial at Woodland

A craggy outcrop of rock on Green Moor, Woodland is engraved with a series of six initials and the name A. Boosey. The initials are H.S., W.R.S., T.S., C.H., M.C. (G?) and RH. A short inscription accompanies them, 'CON OBJECTORS 1916'. The story behind this memorial is still unknown. What were these conscientious objectors doing in Woodland in 1916?

During the Great War, many conscientious objectors joined The Friends' Ambulance Unit, allowing them to participate in the war effort without compromising their faith. Others refused to have any part in the conflict.

Those Excluded From War Memorials

There was one class of men whose names were unwelcome on war memorials, although this has changed in recent years: those who were executed for a variety of military crimes. One man from Sloop Street, Barrow Island, William John Irvine, came under this category.

Lance Corporal William John Irvine, 1st Battalion King's Own, was executed, aged 19, for desertion. He is buried at Le Grand Beaumart British Cemetery, France. Lance Corporal Irvine enlisted on 10 August 1914 and his service number indicates that he was originally a member of the 3rd (Special Reserve) Battalion. Irvine arrived in France on 12 September 1914 and he deserted on 13 October 1914. He was captured and charged with desertion, having stolen goods from a comrade and with escaping after his initial arrest. He was shot at dawn on 20 April 1915.

William John Irvine is not commemorated on any war memorial in Barrow. Whether his mother, Jane, submitted his name for inclusion

Lance Corporal W. J. Irvine's headstone in Le Grand Beaumart British Cemetery. (By kind permission.)

Details of the Irvine Family on the 1911 Census.

on any of the Barrow memorials is not known. His grave is next to that of Private James Kershaw, another deserter from the 1st Battalion, who was shot just six days after Irvine on 26 April 1915.

Another 1st/4th Battalion King's Own man, Private John Sloan, was also executed for desertion on 16 July 1916 and is buried in Barly French Military Cemetery. Over the past 15 years, since the military court martial records have been made public, there have been campaigns by relatives and others, for soldiers executed during the war to be pardoned.

John Sloan's headstone at Barly French Military Cemetery. (By kind permission.)

An Unusual Memorial: Great War Tanks
The celebration of a military victory prompted the acceptance of communities of redundant or captured military hardware. Barrow received a tank, placing it on Biggar Bank (Walney), like nearby Ulverston. The tank had been the latest addition to the weapons of war, and its introduction midway through the Battle of the Somme had appeared to herald a new type of conflict.

The Ulverston Tank in Ellers Square.

Ulverston Council accepted the offer of a trophy field gun, which was placed outside the Ruskin Museum in Coniston. One night, veterans dragged it down to the lake and chucked it in, apparently with the observation that they had seen enough of such things in France. It was raised by local divers in the 1960s.

A Barrow Architect
On 4 November 2013, the Communities Secretary Eric Pickles unveiled the new design of a paving stone intended to commemorate recipients of the Victoria Cross during the First World War. Charlie MacKeith, an architect who works from studios in London and Barrow, was announced as the winner. His design reflects five years of research into memorials, drawing on the experiences of veterans and communities within two Heritage Lottery-funded centenary projects in Preston and Fleetwood.

The design impressed the judges with its elegant simplicity and the stones began being placed in over 400 communities across the United Kingdom in August 2014. The design also incorporates an electronic reader, which people will be able to scan using their smartphones to discover more information about their local Victoria Cross medal recipients.

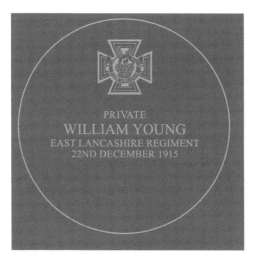

The first paving stone to commemorate a Victoria Cross recipient was laid in August 2014, representing the date when the first two Victoria Cross medals were awarded in the First World War.

CHAPTER 16

Women's War Memorials

Stories of the Great War tend to focus on men. It takes a great deal of effort to see past the servicemen to the women, who have their own wartime stories and also provide examples of heroism. Yet, they do exist, and this chapter tells the stories of some Barrovian women whose wartime stories are worthy of remembrance today.

Women's football team, Barrow.

In Barrow, ground-breaking women workers established one of the first female munitions football teams during the war. On Christmas Day in 1916, a game took place between Ulverston Munitions Girls and another group of local women. Soon, the popularity of women's football inspired by teams like those in Barrow, resulted in huge crowds.

On 21 April 1917, the Workington Munition Girls beat the Carlisle Munition Girls 4-1. On 2 March 1918, women's teams representing Scotland and England competed at Celtic Park. Playing for Scotland were the Beardmore's Munition Girls from Glasgow, who lined up against the Vickers Munition Girls, from Barrow. The game was held to raise money for hospitals, which were then filled with casualties from France. Tickets cost eightpence for the ground and two shillings for the Grand Stand, while wounded soldiers received free admission. England won, with a Miss Dickinson scoring twice. At the end of the First World War, munitionette teams came to an end. Was it difficult for many men to accept the idea of ladies competing in the same sport?

Local Heroines

One Voluntary Aid Detachment (VAD) nurse is mentioned on south Lakeland war memorials, **Sister Tamar Watson** of Ulverston. She died, aged 35, in November 1918, from pneumonia at the Roundhay Military Hospital, in Leeds, where she was on duty. She was buried at Ulverston Cemetery, with full military honours. Sister Watson is not commemorated by the Commonwealth Graves Commission. The circumstances of her death were distressing for her family, as her bereaved parents had recently lost another daughter-in-law and a grandchild to Spanish Flu.

Esther Ellis, a member of the Queen Mary's Auxiliary Corps, has a Commonwealth War Graves Commission-pattern headstone in Barrow Cemetery. This is quite a rarity, as few female war dead are commemorated in the UK.

Esther was under Army orders in the Queen Mary's Army Auxiliary Corps. Their work was

Sister Tamar Watson of Ulverston, was laid to rest with her family. (By kind permission.)

domestic and office work, and it is surmised that she was probably attached to one of the Army Training Schools in Berkhamstead as an office worker – possibly a typist. Many Q.M.A.A.C. lived locally to their work, but a few signed up to work anywhere. It appears that Esther was one of these and that she might have had a special skill that took her so far away from home.

Another local woman, **Jean Battersby** of Carnforth, Lancashire, became a heroine of the First World War. She began her Women's Land Army training on Storey's farm at Bailrigg, Lancaster in May 1917. In February 1918, she went to Warrington to sit 'efficiency tests', which included gardening tests requiring her to bring her own spade. Jean completed the animal husbandry, general labouring and threshing tests, scoring between 80 per cent and 100 per cent in each.

In addition to her high scores, while serving as a Land Girl, Jean was awarded the Cross for Valour, equivalent to the VC for servicemen. Her act of bravery occurred at the Gas Works yard in Carnforth, where a young horse overturned its cart and bolted. At the risk of her own life, she succeeded in stopping the animal.

Esther Ellis worked at the School of Instruction (Berkhampstead) for the Queen Mary's Auxiliary Corps. She died in the UK on 10 December 1918, aged 20.

Ambulance driver **Nellie Taylor** is remembered in Grasmere, a central Lake District village, as a casualty of the First World War. She was a driver with the 10th Motor Ambulance Convoy of the Voluntary Aid Detachment. She died on 27 June 1918 and is buried at Mont Huon Military Cemetery, France. Grasmere War Memorial is some way from St Oswald's Church and it contains no names. These are placed within the church.

Like Nellie, **Agnes Mary Fletcher,** a Grange volunteer nurse, also served overseas during the war. Agnes Mary was educated at Cheltenham Ladies College and Lady Margaret Hall, Oxford. At the time of the 1911 census, she was living at her father's house at Crow How, Ambleside. In June 1915, she was serving at the No 16 General Hospital at Le Treport.

She was mentioned in dispatches for brave conduct by Douglas Haig, who later became the head of Britain's armed forces, on 13 November 1916. She was also recorded as serving at Wimereux and Genoa in Italy.

By February 1919, with the war over, Agnes Mary had returned to England and was working at a military hospital in Weymouth. She was officially demobbed from military hospital service in May 1919. By 1922 she was living with her brother Clement at Atherton, in Manchester. She died on 18 February 1971 and was buried in Atherton Cemetery.

Jean Battersby, Land Girl and recipient of the Cross for Valour. (By kind permission.)

CHAPTER 17

Bitter Sweet Victory

There was relief and joy in towns and cities across Britain on the declaration of the Armistice in November 1918. However, many also remembered those who would not return from the conflict. Most British families would have lost a friend, if not a father, brother, cousin, uncle, in-law or son. War veterans and soldiers at the Front also received the news with mixed feelings.

'Disabled', a poem by Wilfred Owen, explores the effects of war on those who live through it, by comparing the present life of an injured soldier to his past hopes and accomplishments. The women he joined up to impress are ignoring him and he feels that his courage means nothing to them now he is in a wheelchair.

Attitudes had to change. Thomas Hayton Mawson (1861–1933), an architect, was born in Scorton, Lancashire. In 1902, he designed Barrow Park. During World War One, he became concerned about the plight of disabled ex-servicemen and he advanced a scheme for purpose-built villages to house these men . Only one such village, Westfield in Lancaster, was ever built, with the funds raised through private donations. Hayton Mawson died in 1933 at Hest Bank, Lancaster and was buried at Bowness Cemetery, overlooking Lake Windermere.

The Post-War Class System
The pre-war ruling class had considered themselves ideally placed to form the nascent officer class, and many of them saw distinguished war service. By and large they shared the same hardships as their men and, proportionally, the number of officers killed during the war was much higher than the number of other ranks.

The resulting rate of attrition meant that there simply weren't enough ex-public schoolboys to replenish the officer ranks and so the 'Temporary Gentleman' appeared. These were ordinary men, who either had a grammar school education or had shown the requisite leadership skills while serving in the ranks. The latter, in particular, would have earned the respect of their more well-heeled contemporaries, as they had that essential quality experience. A look at the Barrow Grammar School War Memorial indicates just how many middle class local men became officers – and later died.

One of these 'Temporary Gentlemen' was Second Lieutenant Edward Cecil Tootill of the 10th Battalion, Durham Light Infantry. He was killed in action on 22

Old Barrovian Boy's Club member, Second Lieutenant Edward Cecil Tootill.

August 1917, during the Third Battle of Ypres, aged 21, and by that time he had seen more than two years' service at the Front. He was educated at the Barrow Municipal Secondary School, and before the war was articled as a chartered accountant to Messrs. R. F. Miller & Co. He volunteered for service on reaching 19, and entered the Cumberland and Westmorland Imperial Yeomanry.

He was selected for a commission, and went to an officers' training school at Lichfield. He was next gazetted to the Durham Light Infantry and had been in France about five months when he was killed. According to *The Barrovian*: 'He became a member of the Old Boys' Club directly on leaving school and his interest in the doings of the school was shown by his frequent visits to the playing fields.'

Religion

As Barrow had expanded rapidly in its early days, there were insufficient churches and chapels for the growing population. Anglicans were fortunate, in that St George's, St James's, St Paul's and St Matthew's, St Mark's, St Luke's and St John's Churches were all built after generous donations were made by local landowners and industrialists. Not all church-going at this time resulted from a sense of moral and ethical duty, however. There were also social aspects which provided enjoyment for all members of the family.

The twentieth century has seen a great decline in church attendance. Some men returned from the First World War so shattered by the suffering they had experienced that they either rejected Christianity completely, or refused to attend church because of the Anglican Church's general support for the war. There is a notable absence of any religious symbolism on the Cenotaph, the war memorial in London's Whitehall, unveiled in 1920.

APPENDIX I

Diary Extract

Extract from *The Fourth Battalion The King's Own (Royal Lancaster Regiment) and The Great War*, **by Lieutenant-Colonel F. H. A. Wadham and Captain J. Crossley (1935).**

Rue d'Ouvert, 1915

'Rumour, always busy, had for some days prevailed that the 154th Brigade to which we belonged was to be entrusted with an operation more ambitious than usual, and for once rumour was correct. A conference was held at Brigade Headquarters at Locon on the 13th June, and at 7 p.m. the following day the Battalion left billets at Le Cornet Malo, and moved by Companies along the familiar Route C, to take over trenches at Festubert. The transport also moved nearer to the line at Le Touret.

By 10 p.m. the Battalion commenced to arrive in the old British trench, and were all in by 11.30p.m. Contrary to arrangements this trench was already occupied by the 1/6th Scottish Rifles, and room was made in the reserve trench. The intended operation was an attack by the 7th Division, Canadian Division, and our own (the 51st) on the enemy position on the line Chapelle St. Roch-Rue d'Ouvert. After a 48 hours' continuous bombardment our mine at Duck's Bill was fired. At 6 p.m. on the 15th our attack commenced under heavy artillery fire from the enemy. It was led by the 1/4th Loyal North Lancs. on the right, and the 1/6th Scottish Rifles, with the 1/4th King's Own and 1/8th Liverpool (Irish) in support.

'A' Company (less party selected from two platoons under Command of Lieut. R. Gardner for Brigade Relay Posts and less other details) were ordered to occupy and hold Sap L. 8. 'B' Company moved to the old fire trench, and 'C' Company moved forward to take their place in support. 'D' Company moved into support trench, and it was reported that two lines of German trenches had been occupied by 6.20 p.m. 'D' Company were in position at 6.50 when a number of wounded of the 6th Scottish Rifles passed through. At 7.20 all reports from the front were satisfactory. At 8 p.m. 'B' and 'C' Companies were ordered to push on in support of the Loyals and Scottish Rifles, who asked for reinforcements. 'D' were ordered to the fire trench and arrived at 8.25 p.m.

The progress of 'A' Company (less detachment) to Sap L. 8 was delayed by blocks ahead, and bridges broken by shellfire, but they reached their position and performed their allotted duty. 'D' Company moved forward to support the Loyals, and threw back their right flank whilst trying to get into touch with the Grenadier Guards. At 9 p.m. the last platoon of 'D' Company was sent from the reserve trench to rejoin their Company in front. The 8th Liverpools commenced to arrive and moved two Companies to the old fire trench, and one to support. Battalion Headquarters got into touch with the firing line through Lieut. Taylor, the Bombing Officer. Lieut. A. A. Wright, in charge of the Machine Gun Section, was ordered to reinforce the firing line. This move commenced, but could not be completed and the machine guns were buried as the result of enemy shell fire. All the Companies concerned exhibited great gallantry and performed their duties with devotion, and showed fine discipline and steadiness, and excellent fighting qualities. Between 10 and 11 p.m. a retirement was ordered. 'D' Company still tried to establish contact with the Grenadier Guards on our right, but this was not effected until some two hours later.

An Officer of the Loyals reported at Battalion Headquarters about midnight, but could give no clear information of conditions in front. At 12.30 a.m. on the 16th, the German counter-attack was delivered, artillery support was impracticable, heavy casualties had occurred amongst the Officers of the attacking battalions, no supports came up on our right, and our right flank was therefore in peril. Enemy pressure increased, and retirement along the line was effected in good order.

At 1.45 a.m. an order was received to re-form the Battalion in the reserve trench, and a Battalion from the 152nd Brigade moved up in support, the 8th Liverpools taking over the old fire trench. On relief the Battalion assembled at Le Touret at 10 a.m. on the 16th.

A Special Order by Brigadier-General G. L. Hibbert, D.S.O., Commanding the 154th Infantry Brigade was issued as follows: "The Brigadier has received personal instructions from Lieut.-General Sir H. Rawlinson, Commanding IV Corps to convey to the Brigade his appreciation of the gallantry shown by all ranks in the attacks of the 15th and 16th instant under very trying circumstances. The Brigadier wishes to add on his own behalf his appreciation of the pluck and spirit evinced by all and while he deplores the heavy losses incurred congratulates the Brigade on the fine fighting qualities displayed."

The casualties suffered by the Battalion in this action were five officers (three killed, one wounded and prisoner, one wounded) and 147 other ranks (ten killed, 34 wounded and missing, 37 missing and ten sick).'

Rue d'Ouvert, 1914. (By kind permission)

In the dug-outs
Two Barrow friends, Lance Corporal Miller and Corporal T. Timmins, wrote to the *Barrow Evening Mail* in December 1915 from Gallipoli, describing themselves as 'Barrow nuts in a dug-out'. Corporal Timmins wrote:

> As soon as we landed, we were under heavy shell fire and a piece of shrapnel hit the buckle of my belt and turned it inside out; and I can tell you I thought it was my birthday, right enough. But that was not the finish. As I was throwing off my straps I was hit again but it was very low and carried away the heel of my boot. My chum Miller began to laugh at me, but, to his surprise, a bullet caught him fair in the wrist.

Timmins was later sent out as part of a wire-cutting party of 23 men – 18 of them were lost to bullets or shell fire. The rest dug themselves into the ground as best they could and survived a night-long bombardment. Their reward the next morning was what passed for a feast in Gallipoli: 'We got our bully beef and biscuits chopped up and put them into our canteen, and, with a little water, we boiled them, as this was our favourite feed in the dug-outs.'

Research Guidance

- You can explore the **Commonwealth War Graves Commission** database of war deaths on *cwgc.org*. The Forces War Records website, *forces-war-records.co.uk*, was created upon the request of some Forces Reunited members. Here you can order a personalised memorial scroll.

- **War Memorials Online** (*warmemorialsonline.org.uk*) provides an opportunity for users to upload images of war memorials and log concerns for their conservation.

- A printed list of officers taken prisoner was produced during the war and has been reprinted; there is a copy in the library at **The National Archives** in Kew (*nationalarchives.gov.uk*).

- If your ancestor came from Barrow and you want to find out more about him/her, the **Barrow Archive and Local Studies Centre** at 140 Duke Street has many relevant archives. See *Cumbria.gov.uk*

- The *Register of British Conscientious Objectors* compiled by Cyril Pearce, a former lecturer at Leeds University, contains material on more than 17,000 COs. Pearce's material is included on the Imperial War Museum website, *livesofthefirstworldwar.org*.

- The MH 47 series at **The National Archives** contains up to 11,000 case papers from the Middlesex Appeal Tribunal which, between 1916 and 1918, heard appeals from conscientious objectors who had previously applied to a local tribunal for exemption from compulsory military service. These are searchable by name.

- The YMCA's main archive is in the Cadbury Research Library, University of Birmingham, where there is likely to be information about the 'Barrow Hut' for British soldiers. *Being Prepared, 100 Years of Scouting in Cumbria*, Roy McNamara (Bookcase, 2007) also includes information about help on the Home Front.

Newspapers:

Naturally, local and national newspapers are also a major source of information about individuals and events during the First World War. The principal newspapers held by South and West Cumbria Libraries and Archives, which were published during the First World War are:

- *Barrow Guardian* 1910-1947, held at Barrow Archive Centre
- *Barrow News* 1883-1986, held at Barrow Archive Centre
- *Cumberland and Westmorland Herald* 1860-61, 1869, 1873 to date, held at Penrith Library
- *Cumberland News* 1910 to date, held at Carlisle Library
- *Cumberland Pacquet* 1774 – 1915, held at Carlisle, Whitehaven, Workington, Penrith, and Kendal Libraries and Whitehaven Archive Centre
- *Evening News* 1910 to date, held at Carlisle Library
- *Millom Gazette* 1892–1933, held at Barrow and Whitehaven Archive Centres
- *North Western Daily Mail* 1898–1940, held at Barrow Archive Centre
- *Soulby's Ulverston Advertiser* 1848–1914, held at Barrow Archive Centre
- *West Cumberland Times* 1874-1966, held at Workington Library
- *Westmorland Gazette* 1818 to date, held at Kendal Library
- *Whitehaven News* 1856 to date, held at Whitehaven Archive Centre
- *Workington Star* 1904–1967, held at Workington Library

Acknowledgements

I am greatly indebted to several people for lending photographs in their possession and sharing their research with me. Much information has been gleaned from local newspapers and a local historian. And a member of a railway club kindly proofread my information on the Furness Railway. Thanks also to my partner Alan McClenaghan for his computer wizardry with Scrivener and Photoshop and for his help with setting up a promotional website.

Bibliography

Arthur, Max, *Lest We Forget*, (Ebury Press, 2007)

Barnes, Fred, *Industrial Development Handbook, Barrow*, (Grove Publishing Company, 1947)

Classic Boat magazine, Morecambe Bay Prawner, (April 2013)

Cumbria Federation of Women's Institutes, *Cumbria, Within Living Memory*, (Countryside Books, 1994)

van Emden, Richard; Humphries, Steve, *All Quiet on the Home Front: An Oral History of Life in Britain during the First World War*, (Headline, 2003)

Gibson, R. H.; Prendergast, Maurice, *The German Submarine War*, (Naval & Military Press Ltd, 2003)

Gutzke, David W., 'Gender, Class and Public Drinking in Britain during the First World War', *Social History*, Vol. 27, No 54 (1994)

Harris, A., *Cumberland Iron, the Story of Hodbarrow Mine 1855-1968*, (D. Bradford Barton, 1970)

Hutton, J.E., *Welfare and Housing: A Practical Record of Wartime Management* (1918)

Joy, Caroline Anne, 'War and Unemployment in an Industrial Community: Barrow-in-Furness 1914-1926' (Doctoral Thesis, University of Central Lancashire, 2004)

Mitchell, W.R., *Lakeland Dalesfolk (1900-1935)*, (Dalesman Books, 1983)

Marshall, J.D.; Davies-Shiel, M., *The Lake District at Work*, (David and Charles, 1971)

Myers, Bill, *Millom Remembered*, (Tempus, 2004)

Nicholson, Norman, *Wednesday Early Closing*, (Faber and Faber, 1975)

Oliver, Neil, *Not Forgotten,* (Hodder & Stoughton, 2005)

Parker, John, *The Submarine, An Illustrated History from 1900 to 1950*, (Anness, 2008)

Pevsner, Nikolaus, *The Buildings of England, North Lancs*, (Penguin, 1969)

Postlethwaite, Harry, *Transport in Barrow in Furness*, (Venture Publications, 2013)

Roberts, Elizabeth, *Working Class Barrow and Lancaster 1890 to 1930* (University of Lancaster, 1976). [Elizabeth Roberts provides extracts from the transcriptions of her interviews with local people.]

Singleton, Frank, *Lancashire and the Lakes*, (Oliver & Boyd, 1964)

Stevenson, David, *1914 1918, The History of the First World War*, (Penguin, 2004)

Sutherland, Jon; Canwell, Diane, *The Battle of Jutland*, (Pen & Sword, 2007)

Trescatheric, Bryn, *A Shipyard Town* (Self-published, 1994)

Trescatheric, Bryn, *Voices from the Past, Contemporary Accounts of Barrow's History (1870-1939)*, (Self-published, 1994)

Wadham, Lieutenant Colonel F. H. A.; Crossley, Captain J., *The Fourth Battalion The King's Own and The Great War* (1935)

Williams, L.A., *Road Transport in Cumbria in the 19th Century*, (Allen and Unwin, 1975).

Websites:

The Accrington Pals, *http://pals.org.uk*

Airship Heritage Trust, *airshipsonline.com*

British Army website, *army.mod.uk*

Cumbriawarmemorials.blogspot.co.uk

Cumberlandarchives.co.uk

Cumbrian branch of the Western Front Association, (See *westernfrontassociation.com)*

Cumbrianrailways.org.uk

Cumbrianwarmemorials.co.uk

Findagrave.com

Flight.global.com

Lindal and Marton Community website, *lindal-in-furness.co.uk*

Liverpool Daily Post, *liverpooldailypost.co.uk*

The Merchant Navy Association,

Naval Historical Society of Australia, *navyhistory.org.au*

Navalhistory.net

Nicholsonmemorials.org.uk

Pastscape.org.uk

Petergould.co.uk/local_transport

Red-duster.co.uk,

Royalnavy.mod.uk

Southcumbriawarmemorials.webs.com

Workhouses.org.uk

Visitcumbria.com

Index